MW00463757

North Florida
FOLK MUSIC

RON JOHNSON

North Florida
FOLK MUSIC

HISTORY & TRADITION

Charleston  London

THE
History
PRESS

Published by The History Press
Charleston, SC 29403
www.historypress.net

Copyright © 2014 by Ron Johnson
All rights reserved

First published 2014

Manufactured in the United States

ISBN 978.1.62619.580.6

Library of Congress CIP data applied for.

To my parents and my children.

Contents

Foreword

If you go to Webster's dictionary or Wikipedia on the Internet and look up "folk music," you will be as confused as I am on what it's all about. Their conclusion, and mine, is that "despite the assembly of an enormous body of work over some two centuries, there is still no certain definition of what folk music (or even folklore) is, exactly." Our local organization, the North Florida Folk Network (NFFN), and other folk clubs around Florida are constantly grappling with the relevance of the term in this century. In order to appeal to the broadest spectrum of audience, some festivals are dropping the words "folk festival" in favor of "acoustic" or even "Americana" music festival. No doubt, in this book, Ron Johnson will clear up the entire debate for us. Now, if you believe that, I have some swampland I'd like to talk to you about.

I was raised in a musical family in North Carolina, so I was accustomed to folks being passionate about their music (primarily bluegrass) when I moved to Jacksonville, Florida, in 1970. Here in Florida, there was everything from bluegrass to blues, country to southern rock, jazz to pop. Was there any "folk" music? Yes, all of it! That's what folk music is—music of the soul, of the heart, the history, the habits, the culture and the struggles of those telling the tale.

Around North Florida in the '70s, some musicians still in their teens were becoming famous. Many of those folks are familiar to all of us, as they have gone on to international fame and fortune. Ron has the job of making the others familiar to us and connecting the dots of the North Florida music story to the current folk and acoustic music scene in Florida. Along the way,

Ron discovered secrets and solved a few mysteries. You will no doubt be surprised, as you move through these pages, by the variety of musicians who have influenced and have been influenced by Jacksonville and the North Florida music scene. It's an amazing story, really—a story many of us have lived and will always remember. Trying to put it all into words is something else altogether.

Fast-forward to 2014, and we see the spider web network of acoustic/folk musicians, songwriters and entertainers in Florida that I call the "Florida Folk Family." There are more than a half dozen major folk festivals in Florida and dozens of others that celebrate our history, our heritage and our ecology through acoustic music. There is practically a cottage industry of songwriting dedicated to the beauty and diversity of our animals, plant life and folk legends here in the Sunshine State. Those of us fortunate enough to be members of this family treasure our time together as we gather in ever-increasing numbers to share our passion for this great state. Many have dedicated their lives to fight against powerful forces that would destroy the very thing we treasure most. Indeed, many of us are attempting to save Florida through our music. This story, this book you hold in your hands, is about that music, that history and these traditions. Fortunately, Ron Johnson is just the right guide to walk us through this wonderful maze of North Florida folk history!

Singer/songwriter Larry Mangum
Jacksonville, Florida

February 2014

Preface

In 2013, I was approached by The History Press to write a history of folk music in the North Florida region, which initially gave me pause. Why just North Florida? I began to understand as I started writing, however, the full scope of my subject, and my single regret is how much I ended up editing out of the book for the sake of volume and space.

I myself have performed in Florida festivals, including the Florida Folk, Will McLean and Barberville Festivals, for several years now. Before that, I performed mostly solo, just me and my old Epiphone guitar every weekend at a small club in Atlantic Beach, doing covers but sneaking in my originals as much as possible. My musical directions changed radically when I was introduced to the Florida Folk Festival by the Makley family at the fiftieth-anniversary show there. "They've been doing this for fifty years?!" I wondered. "Where have I been?"

Now that I've been performing at some of these festivals and shows for over a decade, I'm no longer considered so much of "a newbie" anymore. In 2011, I won the Will McLean Song Contest (along with Mary Mathews) for the historical tune "Rescue Train," still one of my most requested songs. I've written at least two hundred original songs over the years, most of them turkeys but some good ones, too. I love playing at these festivals and folk shows, and as long as they'll have me, I'll keep showing up. It is an honor rich in tradition, and it is that tradition I am attempting to throw a spotlight on with this book. It still amazes me when I meet people who live in Florida and they tell me they've never heard of Gamble Rogers or Will McLean. I don't know how that happens, and then I remember that for years, I didn't know who they were either—someone had to tell me about them. Hopefully, I can pass some of this insight and awareness about this wonderful music family forward to you.

Just to get it out of the way, my family is from the Crestview/Milton area of the state, and my grandfather raised white face cattle there. His father made his living off turpentine and making roads. My sister Rhonda and several family members still live in that area. I grew up in a navy family, and we moved around a lot, but we spent most of our time in Florida, mostly Jacksonville. I graduated from Nathan Bedford Forrest High School in 1971 (now Westside High School), and for my master's in social work, I went to Florida State University, class of '86. I work in Jacksonville today as a LCSW (licensed clinical social worker).

That's my history and résumé, but for the past decade or so, my history has been deeply interwoven with the Florida folk scene, and I am now a part of it, as surely it is a part of me. Speaking for the moment as the current president of the North Florida Folk Network (NFFN) here in Jacksonville, I am proud to introduce some aspects of that scene and that historical experience to you now.

It strikes me as a little odd to use the written word, a medium without sound, to describe folk music, a medium that depends primarily on sound to be fully appreciated. I encourage my readers to check out the websites of the artists I am presenting here and listen to as many of their songs as possible. I think you'll like what you hear. Many of my friends and "White Springs Nation" family have websites where their CDs and recordings can be purchased. Other websites, including YouTube, ReverbNation and Facebook, offer a glimpse into the great music that is available.

As they say, good live music doesn't go away if you support it.

Acknowledgements

During the writing of this book, the great folk singer, American icon, mentor and father to all folk singers Pete Seeger passed away. No other person influenced folk music as much as Pete did. He was there at the beginning, and he taught us all to sing. He was a beloved giant, and he will be missed.

I need to thank so many people for their help and assistance in this project. As they say, no man goeth alone. First, I need to say thanks to Mr. Frank Thomas, who embodies Florida folk music more than any other person I've ever met. He is a teacher to many, and his patience and mentorship throughout this writing is greatly appreciated. Gratitude to Bob Patterson, who proved to be of great assistance in this writing, as were Larry Mangum, Del Suggs, Tom Shed and Al Poindexter. Thanks to Peter Gallagher, a far better writer than I, for his interviews and stories and Kelly Green for her letter on Stephen Foster. A salute to Mr. Red Henry for his memory and great Gamble Stories, as well as to his son Chris Henry and uncle John Hedgecoth. Thanks, of course, go out to Charlie Robertson and Dale Crider for their patience and insights. We also thank Ruthanne Mason, Lucinda Maynard and Bettina Makley, who contributed much to this project. Love and a big thank you to Margaret Longhill and all the wonderful staff at the Will McLean Foundation for their assistance. Thanks also to Ron and Bari Litschauer, as well as Eroc Hendel and his wonderful family. I am honored that others contributed so much, including John Alison, Emmett Carlisle, Ken and Cee Cee Connors, Ray Lewis, Dennis Devine, Doug Gauss, Jerry Mincey (and his lovely wife, Lynnis), Tony Macaluso, "the Music Man"

Charley Groth, Linda Pottberg, Mike and Maggie McKinney of Lucky Mud, Art and Mary Crummer, James Hawkins, Bill and Eli Perras, Theresa and Bill Ellison, Tim and Karen Bullard (and their very talented daughter Emily Rose), Susan Jean Grandy, Jinx Miller, Bob Lusk, Jim and Carolyn Dunn, Cindy Bear, Ms. Goody Haines, Bobbie Watson, William Conrad, Ken Hodges, Crucial Eddy Cotton, Heather Tanksley, Barry Brogan, Lis and Lon Williamson (and to the whole Gatorbone tribe), Bill Gibson, Doug Purcell, Don Casper, Steve Lowe, Rebecca Zapen-Douglass, Jamie DeFrates and Susan Brown, Benjamin Dehart, Henry Joe Kaiser III, Al Scortino, Paul and Kay Garfinkel, Bob Bronar, Joe and Katie Waller of Jackson Creek, Gloria Holloway, Grant Livingston and especially Elaine McGrath and her wonderful staff at the Stephen Foster Florida State Park. Also a big acknowledgement to Johnny and Jerry Bullard and their wonderful musical family, whose contributions made much of this book a reality. Gamble Roger's family, including Maggie Roberts, Lyn Rogers Lacey, Neely Ann Qualls Miller and Molly Reynolds Gilmer, contributed love and much information. Thanks to Arvid Smith, probably the best musician in the state, and Mary Lee Sweet, of the duo Back In Tyme, who was especially helpful; her knowledge of Florida folk music is vast and encompassing. A poke to my Facebook friends and community for their stories and memories, including Michael Gordon Akers, Mike Johnson, Bob Higginbotham and the great musician and songwriter Jim Carrick.

A great big thank-you goes out to Ron Spencer, my comrade on stage (basically speaking), and much love and acknowledgements to Gail Carson for her spectacular photos, many of whom are included here. She, more than anybody else, is the photographic "eye" of Florida folk and a great songwriter in her own right. I know I have left off a few names, and my memory and notes are failing me right now, so if I left yours or any other deserving name off, please forgive me. All errors are my own.

Love and thanks to my wonderful daughter, Ariel Johnson, for her editing and arranging the index, etc. Thank you, dear. Also to my son, Andrew, who is my joy and inspiration as well. And finally, I am forever indebted to Janice Niemann, whose editing skills, loving assistance and great patience made this book possible.

Introduction

First a word about "folk music" and what it is and isn't. A folk purist might tell you "folk music" is a musical style that emphasizes story telling (i.e., oral traditions). To a musicologist or folklore scholar, the authorship of a true folk song is usually unknown, handed down over the years by the common folk or "the lower classes." Songs like "John Henry" or "Greensleeves" come to mind. Even some children's rhymes that used to be folk songs, such as "Pop Goes the Weasel" and "London Bridge Is Falling Down," might be examples of this strict interpretation. There are thousands more. Under these parameters, they would reject a song like "Home on the Range," which started out as a poem by Dr. Brewster M. Hinley in 1873. The idea that a true folk song has to be anonymous has been argued, but over time, historic investigators have been able to identify authorship on so many songs with some modest success that this has lost some of its weight in defining traditional folk music. Nevertheless, some scholars remain steadfast that if you know who wrote it, it's not technically a "folk song." Happily, it is not a criterion we will be using in this book.

As far as being the "music of the lower classes," I am reminded of Pete Seeger's dad, Charles, who, as a brand-new musicologist out of Harvard, took his young wife and three small sons into the wilds of America's Appalachian Mountains to bring classical music to the poor, uncultured and uneducated people of the Virginias and Carolinas. What this master musician and his classically trained wife quickly discovered was that the common folk had their own music, thank you very much, and they didn't particularly care for any of that high falutin' music from some Julliard professor anyway. Charles

Seeger and his wife were stunned to learn this, but being curious, Charles did in fact stay awhile longer, studying and recording some of this new folk music he had found. His wife, Constance, however, would have nothing to do with it and promptly left him and the children. Surprisingly, it turns out, folk music is not for everybody. Fortunately for the rest of us, a very young Pete Seeger was by his father's side, and he was watching some of those North Carolina banjo pickers real close.

In the end, I think most of us agree "folk music" has always been and always will be music by, for and about the "common people." It certainly does contain an oral tradition in stories of history and culture but also sings about the emotions and feelings, including grief and sorrow, we all have as human beings, as well as the joy, the love and redemption we all experience in our lives. More than any other form of music, folk acknowledges what is good and what is bad about the human condition.

In recent times, folklorists have amended the definition of "folk music" to include the twentieth-century revival of folk music, a branch that first evolved from the New York City scene, especially from the late '50s and early '60s. Alienated by the bomb and the "Red Menace" scare of the '50s, a new generation discovered its own musical roots and began to reinterpret them through younger eyes. Musicians like Pete Seeger, Dave Van Ronk and Ramblin' Jack Elliot began to sing old songs to new ears, and a new revival of folk music took fire. By the time the Kingston Trio; Peter, Paul and Mary; and Bob Dylan arrived, the times were already a-changin'.

That revival influenced an entire generation of young people to pick up guitars, fiddles and banjos to make their own music. In different regions and areas across the country, there were varied results, as one might expect. This book is about the North Florida region only. Other areas of the country have their own distinct, no doubt equally interesting, histories to tell. A book on folk music in South Florida, for example, would be a wonderful read.

In the mid-to-late '60s, this initial folk revival began to wane. The Beatles and a new "pop" music ended folk's reign on the Billboard Top 100. However, the thing about folk music is, it never goes away. Its popularity may ebb and flow, but as long as there's "common" folks around, someone is bound to be playing folk music.

Finally, I will say that writing a history in general is very much like trying to capture the moon by scooping up its reflection in a pond with a leaky bucket. No matter how hard you try to get it right, some of it's going to be wrong. A good historian will spend years researching details to get the facts straight, and inevitably the errors, once published, will reveal themselves to haunt him until the end of his days. In all honesty, this work is not meant to be a scholarly or historical study of any significance. As far as I know, everything I have written here is true to the best of my knowledge. The book is primarily to entertain you, the reader, as I introduce you to the world of folk music in North Florida, as I have come to know it. Nothing more, nothing less. If you enjoy it, I have successfully completed my task.

PART ONE · HISTORY

Florida "Folk" Music Prior
to 1800: Spanish Roots

A s long as there have been folks in Florida, there has been "Florida folk music." Before the Spanish "discovered" Florida in the sixteenth century, Paleo-Indians, dating back some twenty thousand years, sang and chanted songs that people of today will never know. These ancient Floridians would have used these songs to hand down their stories and their histories to their children and to future generations. Over time, some of these songs may have been epic in nature, long and quite complex. They were singing the folk music of their time.

In 1513, Juan Ponce de León sailed from Puerto Rico looking for new slaves and new real estate to conquer. Credited with discovering the Gulf Stream, Juan and his three ships landed somewhere on the east coast of Florida and declared it "La Florida" in honor of the Easter holiday weekend, which the Spanish called *Pasque Florida* or "Festival of Flowers."

Did the Timacua Indians greet the Spanish conquistador with a few folk songs of their day? If they did, Juan must not have been overly impressed, for he stayed only a few days and then promptly left. Sailing back south and around Florida to its west coast, he landed near modern-day Tampa. Instead of greeting him and his troops with folk songs, the Calusa Indians, not known to be a particularly friendly bunch, shot darts into Juan, which eventually killed him by the time he was able to make it back to Cuba. This event is looked on by some Floridians as the first "tourist season."

In the next few decades, Spanish explorers began to trickle in. In 1528, Pánfilo de Nárvaez landed in the Tampa area looking for gold and souls to convert. In May 1539, the brutal Hernando de Soto landed on the west

Juan Ponce de León.
Anonymous sixteenth-
century painting. *Image
No. RC09544. State
Archives of Florida,*
Florida Memory,
*http://floridamemory.com/
items/show/32329.*

coast of Florida and set off to explore the new land, killing off entire tribes of Indians along the way. The local indigenous peoples would have Florida to themselves for a couple decades more, but it was becoming increasingly evident that the Spanish and Europeans were coming, and things would never be the same.

Although the Spanish had claimed La Florida for their own, ironically, the earliest record of what could possibly be considered a Florida folk song was not by the Spanish but by the French, or more specifically, the French Huguenots. The Huguenots were Protestants and were viewed as heretics by the Spanish Catholics.

French Huguenots under the guidance of Jean Ribault had already established a colony in South Carolina in 1562, and two years later, Ribault attempted to settle Fort Caroline near present-day Jacksonville in 1564 with René Laudonnière. The French lived in northern Florida for almost two years, and had they stayed, Jacksonville (and not St. Augustine) might have been known as the nation's oldest city.

The French, it seems, were quite musical and taught the local Indians many of their hymns. Most of these were written by Martin Luther himself and would have been sung along the banks of the modern-day St. John's River as they worked or in their house of worship on the Sabbath. These hymns would have included "To Jordan Came the Christ Our Lord," "From Depths of Woe I Cry to You" and "Come Holy Spirit."

It seems appropriate, then, that the earliest folk song ever written about Florida was composed by the French. It is actually an extant poem written down by Thomas Colwell in the *Stationers' Register* in 1564 and presented in an excellent literary collection of Florida folk songs, *Folksongs of Florida*, by Alton C. Morris. This is exactly how it was written down by Thomas Colwell, almost five hundred years ago, reflecting the language of the time:

The Preme Rose In The Grene Forest

Have you not hard of Floryda,
A countree far by west?
Where savage pepell planted are
By nature and by best,
Who in the mold fynd glysterynge gold
And yt for tryfels sell:
With hy!

Ye, all along the water syde,
Wher yt doth eb and flowe
Are turkeyse found, and wher also
Do perles in oysters grow;
And on the land do cedars stand
Whose bewty do excell.
With hy! Wannot a wallet do well?

The French Huguenots were well versed in the arts and music but not so much in the art of warfare, it seems. When the Spanish caught wind that the French were settling into North Florida, they sent Pedro Menéndez from Cuba to evict them. Menéndez established St. Augustine on August

28, 1565, as a military post for this operation and began setting up camp. Unprepared and vulnerable, Menéndez and his men were caught off guard by the cunning Jean Ribault as his war ships appeared one by one over the horizon.

Unfortunately for the French, Mother Nature had a few surprises of her own, and a hurricane suddenly appeared (no Doppler radar back then!). As the French ships moved toward St. Augustine, the winds and rain were upon them. The great storm sank Ribault's ships, and his troops either drowned in their heavy armor or were washed up and scattered along the beaches south of St. Augustine, barely alive.

Wasting no time, Menéndez and his men marched up to Fort Caroline, where they attacked the unprotected fort and wiped out the settlers there. A few, including René Laudonnière, managed to escape. Menéndez quickly returned to St. Augustine and rounded up the surviving Huguenot soldiers on the beaches to the south. The French attempted to surrender, but the Spanish would have none of that, and the remaining Huguenots fell under the Spanish knives, including the famous Jean Ribault. Today, the area where they died is now known as *Matanzas*, the Spanish word for slaughter.

In time, as more and more Europeans arrived, the Indians, who initially couldn't tell a Frenchman from a Spaniard, needed a way to determine who was who in this deadly conflict. The Indians learned to sometimes screen Europeans when they first met them by humming a few bars of the French songs they had been taught earlier. If the white European knew the song, he was obviously French, and depending on the loyalties of the Indian, he would either be welcomed or killed outright on the spot—a sort of deadly variation to *Name That Tune*!

With the demise of Fort Caroline and the French out of the way for now, the Spanish kept a loose but guarded approach to Florida, maintaining its sovereignty over the land but, with the exception of certain towns, never really settling Florida en masse.

In the Spanish courtyards of St. Augustine and Pensacola, Spanish music included the zarzuela, a sort of opera-lite, which continues to this day. Eventually, Flamenco music and dancing were introduced as early as the 1780s, as well as the Jota dancers with their castanets, spinning to the rhythms and beats of the music.

With rare exceptions, the modern ear would have recognized very little in the music played in Florida back then. One of these exceptions would have been the tune "Greensleeves." It predates *William Ballet's Lute Book* (published around 1580) and is usually associated with the English but actually may be of Italian origin. Regardless of its true beginnings, the song would have certainly been played by wandering musicians along Florida's old Spanish trail or in the towns.

There is no doubt that Spanish tunes were the predominant music in the Sunshine State for over 250 years, all throughout the sixteenth and seventeenth centuries. Most of those influences began to fade as the British and Americans started to make their presence known from the thirteen colonies to the north. After some horse trading back and forth between the Spanish and Brits, Florida fell into American hands in 1819, but even today, especially in South Florida and Miami, contemporary Spanish and Latino music remains an active scene. Artists like Gloria Estefan and Juan Luis Guerra are keeping this tradition of what is actually Florida's longest reign of folk music very much alive.

Stephen Foster: The Father of American Music

Stephen Foster was the first American pop star—the first musician to sell over one million units, measured then in sheet music sales. He was the first real American songwriter and still one of the country's greatest musical talents of all time.

Foster was born on July 4, 1826, fifty years to the date of our nation's founding. He was raised in an affluent, upper-middle-class family in Pennsylvania, mostly in Pittsburgh. As a young man, Stephen learned his way around the piano and showed a flair for performing and writing songs even as a child. After a less than spectacular academic career, Foster worked as a clerk in his brother's steamboat business in Ohio. By the mid-1830s, however, he was beginning to find some modest success in his real passion: writing songs for minstrel shows.

Minstrel shows, by this time, were all the rage, especially in the cities. Beginning in 1843, these theatre groups were able to say things in a way that would have been impossible using other musical styles and venues. With such groups as the Virginia Minstrels, these spirited shows were a direct contrast to the structured restraints of opera, formal theatre (which most folks couldn't afford anyway) and the solemn church hymns of the time.

To contrast this highly restrictive musical structure of the day, minstrel shows emerged featuring blackface performers who were free to express themselves through humor and slapstick but also through a more upbeat, lively song and dance routine that was almost contagious. Characters like Old Jim Crow and Zip Coon were able to say things and perform in ways no

Portrait of Stephen Foster (1826–1864). *Public Domain. Image No. FP79832. State Archives of Florida,* Florida Memory, *http:// floridamemory.com/items/ show/115270.*

respectable person, black or white, ever could. Songs like "Old Dan Tucker" and "Turkey in the Straw" would always arouse an enthusiastic response from the crowd.

Stephen Foster was very much caught up in the raw energy of these minstrel shows, and trying his own hand at the sport, wrote several songs including "De Camptown Races" and "Oh, Susanna!" This latter tune became an anthem for the Forty-niners who participated in the gold rush of 1848–85. As big as that song was in sheet music sales, with over one million units sold, Foster collected only $100 in royalties.

Foster published his first collection of songs, *Foster's Ethiopian Melodies,* in 1849, and almost immediately several minstrel companies began performing them. In September 1849, Foster signed a publishing contract with New York's Firth, Pond & Co. guaranteeing a royalty of 8 percent, about two cents per copy of sheet music sold (around twenty-five cents in 2014 values). Encouraged and with money finally trickling in, Stephen married Jane McDowell, the daughter of a Pittsburgh physician, on July 22, 1850.

Stephen Foster as a lad, around 1835. *Public Domain. Image No. FN00065. State Archives of Florida,* Florida Memory, *http://floridamemory.com/items/show/115060.*

Edwin Pearce "E.P." Christy, a well-known balladeer who had one of the most popular troupes in New York City, the Christy Minstrels, picked up several of Foster's tunes to perform in his shows and asked Stephen for an exclusive contract. Thrilled, Foster resigned his position of clerk at his brother's company in Ohio and announced he was now going to be a professional songwriter.

As there was no such thing as a "professional songwriter" before Stephen Foster, his wife was understandably skeptical. Fortunately, E.P. Christy was a fair-minded businessman (fairer than most music publishers, anyway), and he presented Stephen with $15,000 plus royalties for exclusive rights to his future songs, an enormous fee even back then. One can easily imagine that Foster's wife felt reassured that this might work out after all. Unfortunately, in the long run, it did not.

"Old Folks at Home" is the song that ties Stephen Foster to Florida, even though it almost didn't happen. The story goes that when Foster was writing the original lyrics, he was uncertain about which river he wanted to include in the song. He had never been to the South and didn't really know the

"Gone to Alabama." Lithograph of a poster for the Christy Minstrels. *Lithograph by Napoleon Sarony and Henry B. Major. Oliver Ditson Publisher, 1847. Public Domain.*

geography that well, so he took down an atlas, and with his brother assisting him, they began looking for the names of rivers he might be able to use. They considered the Yazoo River in Mississippi, but Foster quickly dismissed it. His brother liked the name of the Pee Dee River, which flows through both the Carolinas, but Foster laughed out loud at that one. Reading off a list of names, Foster's brother finally stumbled on a little river that flowed south out of Georgia, through Florida and into the Gulf. When his brother spoke the words "Suwannee River," Foster is said to have exclaimed, "That's it exactly!"

In presenting the song to E.P. Christy, however, Foster wondered if it might taint or even ruin his career as a songwriter. He asked Christy to put his own name on it as the author to protect Foster from any political fallout he might experience, although it didn't stop him from asking the music publisher to pay him royalties for the work anyway. Christy, recognizing the song for what it was, was more than happy to agree. After the song became as popular as it did, Foster reconsidered and went back to Christy a year later, asking that his name be put back on the sheet music as its author. This time, Christy was not too happy with Foster's waffling and hesitated for another year before finally putting Foster's name on the sheet music. This odd transaction began to sour their business relationship, and Foster eventually fell out of favor with his benefactor. For two years, Christy's sheet music claimed authorship, and there are collectors today who still look for "Old Folks at Home" by E.P. Christy.

To the modern ear, the lyrics of "Old Folks at Home" appear hopelessly out of date:

> *Way down upon de Swanne Ribber,*
> *Far, far away,*
> *That's where my heart is turning eber,*
> *That's where de old folks stay...*
> *Oh, darkies, how my heart grows weary...*

Seen as racist today, one must remember this was 1851, and abolitionists who railed against the two-hundred-year-old institution of slavery in the United States were still considered radical. As hard as it is to believe today, many whites simply viewed blacks as sub-human, more like animals, cattle or property. Some even argued Negroes were incapable of feeling emotions and pain the way whites did. It is well documented that Foster was sympathetic to the abolitionists' cause, but as a songwriter for minstrel shows, what could he do about it?

It is here that the real power of folk songs is revealed. In addition to comedy and skits, Foster introduced to the minstrel shows music and lyrics that evoked strong emotions and feelings of sympathy for these Negro slaves (although, ironically, the actors themselves were always white with black paint on their faces). Songs like "Hard Times Come Again No More" and "Old Folks at Home" were written not for laughter but to stir something deeper in the soul, some sad nostalgic emotion that we all could empathize with as human beings. Who would not feel sympathy for the blackfaced actor as he sang in a beautiful sad voice how much he missed "the old folks at home"? Listening with our modern ears, we forget that "Old Folks at Home," in its vast popularity, became an instrument that helped chip away at the very foundation of this evil institution of slavery that Foster hated. Harriet Beecher Stowe, influenced herself by Stephen Foster's music, would later, in 1852, write her famous novel *Uncle Tom's Cabin*, which helped humanize the slave in America and abroad, reportedly making the Queen of England cry when she read it.

Far from celebrating the traditions of the old southern plantations and its slaves, "Old Folks at Home" and Foster's songs that followed, began to help whites perceive slaves as genuine people, with the same emotions and feelings that they had. Fredrick Douglass remarked that Stephen Foster's songs were beginning to "awaken sympathies for the slave." Maintaining the institution of slavery under such a growing social awareness was becoming more and more difficult. Foster's songs added fuel to the fire of the political argument of his day, an argument that only ten years later would erupt into a great civil war that would tear the country apart. Ironically, although he helped bring it about in his way, Foster never lived to see a slave-free America.

After 1851, Stephen Foster continued to write songs and had a long stream of sheet music hits, including "My Old Kentucky Home," "Old Black Joe," "Hard Times Come Again No More," "Old Dog Tray," "Angelina Baker" and "Jeanie with the Light Brown Hair," which he wrote for his wife.

Unfortunately, Foster's marriage was now on the rocks, and he felt a change in venue might be helpful, so he and his family, which now included a young daughter, moved to New York City in 1860, just prior to the Civil War. Foster's wife, Jane, was unhappy, and she hated New York, but she especially hated her husband's drinking. By 1861, she had had enough, so she took their daughter and returned to their home in Pittsburgh. By now, any money Foster had managed to make was beginning to run out, and the quality of his newer songs never matched the magic of what he had written before.

Stephen Foster (1859). *Public Domain. Image No. RC11237. State Archives of Florida,* Florida Memory, *http://floridamemory. com/items/show/33781.*

In 1863, he began working with George Cooper, who specialized in comedic lyrics, but the times were a-changing, and the Civil War brought a new demand for patriotic marching songs, which were the rage. Minstrel shows were becoming passé, and in his last years, Foster composed some spirituals and Sunday school hymns, including "Give Us This Day" in 1863.

The year 1863 was a bad one for Stephen Foster. He had no more hits, and even though people still continued to play his songs in homes and parlors across the country, he was seeing no monies from it. Impoverished, living off the small loans he could get from his brother and friends, Foster stayed in the cheap North American Hotel at 30 Bowery in Manhattan. In the winter months, he fought off a flu that wouldn't go away and was confined to his bed with a fever all through Christmas that year. On the morning of January 10, 1864, he called for a chambermaid, but when she didn't come, he attempted to get up on his own. He collapsed and knocked over a washbasin next to his bed, shattering it. He fell down and managed to gouge his forehead with a piece of the porcelain. With the help of a friend, he made his way to Bellevue Hospital, but infection quickly set in, and since there were no antibiotics then, Stephen Foster died three days later, on January 13, 1864, at age thirty-seven.

In his wallet, they found a piece of paper with the words "Dear friends and gentle hearts." He had thirty-eight cents to his name in Civil War scrip and three copper pennies. After his death, his last composition was published, a new song he had written, called "Beautiful Dreamer":

> *Beautiful dreamer, wake unto me,*
> *Starlight and dewdrops are waiting for thee;*
> *Sounds of the rude world, heard in the day,*
> *Lull'd by the moonlight have all pass'd away!*
> *Beautiful dreamer, queen of my song,*
> *List while I woo thee with soft melody;*
> *Gone are the cares of life's busy throng,*
> *Beautiful dreamer, awake unto me!*
> *Beautiful dreamer, awake unto me!*

Foster was buried in his beloved Pittsburgh, on the grounds of the Allegheny Cemetery. The "Father of American Music," who had written over two hundred of America's finest songs, died a pauper and a broken man, a drunk who lived alone on the Bowery. Fortunately, time has been more kind to Stephen Foster than his final years were.

Did Foster Ever Visit Florida?

In the singular moment Foster exclaimed that the Suwannee River was "it exactly," he managed to change Florida's future forever. His decision sent things into motion that ended not only with the song being designated as the state song of Florida in 1935 but also with the establishment of the Stephen Foster Park in White Springs, Florida, in 1950, the site of the annual Florida Folk Festival. However, as most historians will tell you, Stephen Foster himself never set foot in Florida and never visited the Suwannee River.

Or did he?

For many years, stories would be told by the residents along the Suwannee River that Foster had indeed visited that area, at a time when the steamboats ran all the way up the river from the Gulf to the town of Ellaville. Stories

Steamboat Louisa *up the Suwannee River in the 1880s. Public Domain. Image No. RC03844. State Archives of Florida,* Florida Memory, *http://floridamemory.com/items/show/27421.*

from reliable sources have suggested Foster made the trip up the river and sat and had at least a couple drinks with the locals. Of course, it would seem only natural that tall tales and wishful thinking might be a part of Stephen Foster's legend, but in a letter dated April 2003 and written by J.L. McMullen of Live Oak (see Appendix B), he suggests that there may be more to these tall tales than one might assume.

McMullen's family had lived in this area for many generations, and he himself served as the county clerk of the state circuit court from 1937 to 1949. He served on many local boards, including the Stephen Foster State Park, and McMullen was very much involved in getting the first Florida Folk Festivals off the ground. In this letter, he cites a story by Aubrey Fowler, suggesting it was his own grandfather Fowler who "shared a home brew with Stephen Foster" at the country store on the east bank of the Suwannee River. The small country store was then owned by Bud O'Hara and is still located at that site, although it is dilapidated, run down and has been inactive now for many years. The letter also cites a nephew of Bud O'Hara, who suggests his family passed down a narrative over the years relating how Foster visited Ellaville, where the family store was located.

Of course, any possible eyewitnesses are long gone, and at best this evidence is hearsay—secondhand information handed down through the generations. However, it does raise an interesting possibility: could it have happened?

Let us consider the facts: Did Stephen Foster ever get close enough to even visit the Suwannee? He did. He honeymooned in New Orleans, a two-day boat ride away. Foster married Jane Denny McDowell on July 22, 1850. Since we know "Old Folks at Home" was first published in 1851, it would be natural to assume that Foster had no reason to visit the Suwannee during his honeymoon, since he didn't pick the name of the river in his song until 1851, a year after his marriage.

Except that we have to remember that Stephen and his bride waited and took a delayed honeymoon in 1852. It was a month-long steamship ride to New Orleans with friends, the only trip Stephen ever made to the Deep South. By 1852, of course, "Old Folks at Home" was a huge sheet music hit. While he honeymooned a mere boat ride away from the subject of what would be his greatest song ever, one has to ask: how could he not go? And if it was his honeymoon, did his wife happen to come along as well?

Could it have happened? The historical time line of known events makes it a remote possibility, although to date there is no real, hard evidence to suggest he actually did. Without a signed receipt, guest ledger or lost steamboat record with Stephen's name or signature on it showing he visited Florida, no real proof exists, and that is that. I do suggest, however, that it certainly deserves further research and is no doubt an intriguing topic for another day.

Whether he ever visited this region or not, Stephen Foster certainly changed Florida history forever. Foster's legacy continues throughout the Sunshine State, as well as the rest of the country, to this day.

3

The 1860s to 1900: A Not-So-Civil War

After twenty-five years of being only a colony, on March 3, 1845, Florida finally became a state and joined the Union for the first time. Florida landowners and settlers were thrilled. Ironically, in a mere fifteen years, they couldn't wait to get back out again.

THE BONNIE BLUE FLAG

North Florida does have an association with one of the most memorable songs to come out of the early years of the Civil War, "The Blue Bonnie Flag." In 1810, the United States and Spain had a dispute over a large section of western Florida and some of Louisiana as well. Spain declared it its land, but the United States felt it was included in the Louisiana Purchase. A group of settlers who lived there took matters into their own hands and declared the land the "Republic of West Florida." When the United States annexed the territory, it didn't recognize the defiant West Florida government, and after a few words were exchanged (including verbal threats of war), eventually the "little territory that could" gave in and disbanded itself.

The flag that flew over the Republic of West Florida was a solid blue field with a single white star on it, the Bonnie Blue Flag. Some of these settlers swore they were ready to die for their new flag and country, and it was widely recognized then and forever as "that rebel flag."

Fifty years later, in January 1861, Mississippi joined South Carolina and broke away from the Union, declaring itself a free state. The Mississippi politicians decided to fly this rebel flag, the Bonnie Blue Flag, over the Capitol Dome in Jackson, and it became recognized as the unofficial flag for the new and emerging Confederacy. This flag was replaced two months later when the "Stars and Bars" was unveiled as the official flag in the new nation's capital in Montgomery, Alabama. Emotions were running high during this time, and Harry MacCarthy, being the good songwriter that he was, took advantage of this sentiment and composed the song "The Bonnie Blue Flag (We Are a Band of Brothers)." It was an enormous hit in sheet music sales and became the first unofficial anthem for the new Confederacy.

The song was first performed by MacCarthy in the spring of 1861 at a concert in Jackson, Mississippi. He performed it again at the New Orleans Academy of Music that same year. The A.E. Blackmar Music Publishing Company in New Orleans issued six separate editions of "The Bonnie Blue Flag" during the war, including at least three additional arrangements. These were the lyrics MacCarthy wrote:

> *We are a band of brothers and native to the soil!*
> *Fighting for our Liberty, With treasure, blood and toil!*
> *And when our rights were threatened, the cry rose near and far,*
> *Hurrah for the Bonnie Blue Flag that bears a single star!*
> *Chorus:*
> *Hurrah! Hurrah!*
> *For Southern rights, hurrah!*
> *Hurrah for the Bonnie Blue Flag that bears a single star!*

In the 1939 classic film *Gone with the Wind*, Rhett Butler names his daughter Bonnie Blue Butler after he notes the child's eyes are as "blue as the Bonnie Blue flag."

There was plenty of music and songs that came out of the Civil War, and as troops moved about on land and sea, soldiers and sailors in Florida would have surely sung them. When the war was new and hopes remained high, songs like "Dixie" and, for the North, "When Johnny Comes Marching Home Again" reflected the patriotism of the day. Both sides assumed the war would be only a "ninety-day war," and folks like William Tecumseh Sherman, who suggested the fighting might possibly go on "for years," were considered quite mad.

During these bloody years, both sides had their bands and musicians who followed them into battle and encampment, where they played many of the troop's favorites. The Union troops sang "Battle Cry of Freedom," "John Brown's Body" (which later became "The Battle Hymn of the Republic") and "Marching Through Georgia." The Southern men crooned "Dixie," of course, along with "The Yellow Rose of Texas" and "We Are Going to the Wars, Willie Boy!" Stephen Foster's songs were still being played, of course, but by then these tunes were already considered a bit old-fashioned.

During the war, hundreds of songs emerged, played in every corner of the nation, as we killed and slaughtered one another with a vengeance. After 1863, songs began to change their tempo and mood as newspapers reported the long lists of those killed in battle after battle and more and more bodies came home. Songs from that era include "The Vacant Chair" and "When This Cruel War Is Over."

In Florida, there were a fair number of skirmishes and challenges, but fewer than in many other states. The biggest battle fought in Florida was the Battle of Olustee (or Ocean Pond). On February 20, 1864, in the piney woods a good half-day's march outside Jacksonville, General Truman Seymour's Union army of 5,500 men faced off with 5,000 Confederates under General Joseph Finegan. The fighting lasted for almost four hours and was particularly vicious and brutal. As this was near the end of war, very few prisoners were taken, and Negro soldiers in particular could expect no mercy from hardened, bitter Southern troops. Over 2,000 men died or were wounded there, including some of the black troops from the famous Fifty-fourth Regiment, Massachusetts Volunteer Infantry, who were highlighted in the 1989 movie *Glory*.

As one might expect, the Battle of Olustee is a common theme in modern-day Florida folk songs, and there have been many tunes written about this historical event, including Frank Thomas's excellent version, "The Battle of Olustee" from his *Florida Stories* album. Another Florida folk CD highlighting this battle is Brian Smalley's excellent folk-opera *Chicken/Pigs*, which covers a Florida family during the entire war. In his version, a frightened soldier climbs up high in a pine tree and observes the battle down below. When the soldier descends, he is arrested and sent to a Confederate prison.

There were of course other battles in Florida, and there are songs about those as well. Frank Thomas also does a great song about the Battle of Natural Bridge, an 1865 battle near Tallahassee that involved teenaged military cadets, wounded soldiers from the nearby hospital and older veterans. This rag-tag group managed to bottleneck John Newton's Union

troops at a natural bridge on the St. Mark's River. The Union troops retreated, and Tallahassee had the distinction of being the only capital east of the Mississippi in the Confederacy that was never captured by Union troops. The teenage military cadets were students from the Florida Military and Collegiate Institute in Tallahassee, which later became Florida State University. Some of these students were wounded and recognized for bravery, and the Battle of Natural Bridge has sometimes been referred to as "the Battle of FSU," especially by Florida State University alumni.

By war's end, the robust, boisterous songs of a once proud South were now "gone with the wind," and the music that followed was primarily songs of sadness, sorrow, loss and tragedy. Hymns and gospel songs were relied on to lift the burden of defeat as carpetbaggers and Northerners came south to take advantage of the defeated nation. These were hard times, and it would be years before Southerners could celebrate the Fourth of July again.

On a national level, events in American folk music after the Civil War include the 1867 publication of *Slave Songs of the United States* by William Francis Allen, considered by musicologist and author Gilbert Chase to be a "milestone not just in African American music but in modern folk history." It is the first published collection of African American music of any kind and includes such songs as the earliest version of "Michael, Row Your Boat Ashore."

Above: Monument for the Battle of Natural Bridge Battlefield. *Image No. RC11665. Used with permission. State Archives of Florida*, Florida Memory, *http://floridamemory.com/items/show/34143.*

Opposite: The Fifty-fourth Massachusetts Regiment at the Battle of Olustee, by A. Kurz and Alison. *Lithograph print, circa 1900. Public Domain. Florida State Library.*

Some of the popular songs of the day that would have made their way down to Florida included "My Grandfather's Clock" by Henry Clay Works in 1875, a song that not only sold over one million music sheets but also started a big boom in tall, stand-up grandfather clocks. Another popular song during this time was "Home on the Range," a romanticized version of the West, written originally as a poem by Dr. Brewster Higley and officially adopted as the state song of Kansas in 1947. Despite its famous lyrics, there are no actual antelope species native to the Americas (although the pronghorn is often referred to incorrectly as an antelope).

In 1888, the American Folklore Society was formed, modeled after the Folklore Society of Britain, and was "dedicated to gathering and publishing the folk songs and stories of North America."

Around 1897, a new type of music called "the blues" was becoming popular, introduced through such early artists as Henry Sloan and Charlie Patton. Sloan's name is not as well known, but it is reported he taught and mentored Patton, who went on to become known as "the Father of the Delta Blues."

THE SPANISH-AMERICAN WAR

It would take a threat from foreigners and another war to bring us back together as a nation, and in the late 1890s, we got just that. The United States had decided to intervene in the revolution in Cuba to the point that the battleship USS *Maine* was blown up in Havana's harbor on February 15, 1898. Who did it? Some say the Spanish, some say the rebels and some say the Americans themselves did it. In the end, it didn't really matter, as we were all a nation once again, a united people facing a common foe. The press didn't bother to report the fact that more soldiers died from the mosquitoes that carried malaria and yellow fever and, sadly, from the contamination of the army's own tin food rations, but ten weeks later, the fighting was done, and our "splendid little war," as Secretary of State John Hay called it, was over. Teddy Roosevelt was our new national hero, and in 1901, he was selected to be vice-president under newly elected William McKinley. When McKinley was assassinated, the forty-two-year-old Roosevelt became the youngest president of the United States.

The Spanish-American War actually produced a few patriotic songs, nothing too memorable but worthy of our attention here. Many of these songs are listed in John Kendrick Banks's book *Spanish-American War Songs*, and one of my favorites is this little ditty called "A Wise Girl":

When Willie in the regiment
Went out to meet the foe,
His sweetheart stood with face intent,
And pale to see him go.
Though sank her heart within her breast,
She did not dare to cry,
She heard in wartime it was best
To keep your powder dry.

By the end of the nineteenth century, America was changing fast. New innovations were beginning to emerge as Americans found their footing again. Optimism was high in the North, less so in the South, but there was no doubt in anyone's mind the future was upon them as they looked into the rapidly approaching twentieth century.

One new invention in particular, the Edison phonograph player, was about to change the way America listened to and recorded music forever.

4

Music in Florida from 1900 through World War II

A t the beginning, Edison's recording machines were simply cylinders wrapped in tin foil with the sounds scratched on the surface, but they were considered nothing less than magic when they first appeared. Trying to avoid the concept that they were novelty items only for the rich, Edison vowed to "put a gramophone in every American household," and he worked at making the new medium easy to use and affordable.

The technology in recorded music evolved swiftly and moved out of the hands of Edison to bigger companies. Recorded music went from aluminum foil wrapped around a tube to more sophisticated cylinders and, very soon after that, to wax discs. In 1908, Columbia Records introduced mass production of disc records with recordings pressed on both sides, which soon became the industry standard. Patrons of disc records could now get two recordings for less than the price of one cylinder. Eventually, even Edison abandoned the cylinders in favor of the discs when he formed Edison Disc Records.

Popular recordings back in the late 1800s and into the new century included the classics and operas, brass marching bands, ragtime and jazz, comedy, vaudeville sketches, church hymns and Tin Pan Alley songs. The first million-seller was Enrico Caruso, the famous Italian tenor. Amazingly, Caruso made approximately 290 commercially released records from 1902 to 1920, 20 of them selling over one million units. All of Enrico's recordings, which span most of his stage career, are still available today on CDs and as digital downloads.

In North Florida at the turn of the century, phonograph players and records were rare but were becoming more popular, especially in towns like Jacksonville, Cedar Key and Pensacola.

THE MUSICOLOGISTS

Musicologists and collectors of folklore history saw the new recording medium for what it was and immediately went to work. People like Charles Seeger (Pete's father) began recording "hillbilly music" in the Carolinas, and John and Alan Lomax recorded "cowboy songs" out west. In Florida, Jacksonville native Stetson Kennedy, alongside writer Zora Neale Hurston and a young University of Florida intern, Alton C. Morris, were all involved in recording folk singers, blues musicians and storytellers throughout northern Florida and South Georgia.

John Lomax

John Lomax not only collected recordings for the government when Franklin Roosevelt came into power under the New Deal, but he also put many of the old songs in several books that became standards for folk singers at that time, including his 1934 *American Ballads and Folk Songs*.

In July 1933, while visiting the Louisiana State Penitentiary, Lomax met Hudie Ledbetter, aka "Lead Belly," who played a twelve-string guitar and had a distinct, low, mournful sound. Lead Belly was later released from prison and became John's personal driver, taking him to lectures and performances, which he joined in on. After six months on the road, the two quarreled, and even though they never spoke again, Lead Belly's relationship with John's son Alan continued for many years afterward. In 1934, John Lomax became the honorary consultant and curator of the Archive of American Folk Song, a position he held until his death in 1948. In 1942, Harold Spivacke, the chief of the Library of Congress's Division of Music, wrote:

> *Many hard-working and expert folklorists cooperated in the accumulation of this material, but in the main the development of the Archive of American Folk Song represents the work of two men, John and Alan Lomax. Starting in 1933, the Lomaxes, father and son, traveled tens of thousands of miles, endured many hardships, exercised great patience and tact to win the confidence and friendship of hundreds of singers in order to bring to the Library of Congress records of the voices of countless interesting people they met on the way. Very much remains to be done to make our Archive truly representative of all the people, but the country owes a debt of gratitude to these two men for the excellent foundation laid for future work in this field.*

Alan Lomax

It can be said that more than any other single person, Alan Lomax helped influence and create the modern-day folk revival of the twentieth century in America.

Having worked alongside his father for over fifteen years, John's son Alan Lomax not only continued in his father's footsteps but also took the task of recording American folk music to new levels. Alan continued working for the Library of Congress until 1942, when the program was closed. During this time, Alan made tens of thousands of records, including the first "man on the street" interviews.

In 1935, Alan came to Florida, where he worked with a team to record migrant workers and gather a collection of old folk songs. His team included Zora Neale Thurston, who later wrote the 1937 novel *Their Eyes Were Watching God*, and civil rights champion Stetson Kennedy, who was working for the Works Progress Administration at that time. Together with folklorist Mary Elizabeth Barnicle and University of Florida internist Alton C. Morris, they traveled to collect music from the Georgia Sea Islands and along the Florida coast.

After the WPA closed the program in 1942, Alan Lomax went on to record many folk singers who became nationally known, including Woody Guthrie, Burl Ives, Josh White and Pete Seeger, among others. In 1940, Alan produced two groundbreaking albums for RCA records, which have been referred to as the first concept albums, including *Woody Guthrie's Dust Bowl Ballads* and Lead Belly's *Midnight Special and Other Southern Prison Songs*.

Alan spent his whole life recording songs and interviews, speeches and events, as well promoting folk concerts in the United States. He released several anthologies and folk collections that are now considered classics. In 1986, Alan received the National Medal of Arts from President Ronald Reagan, and his 1993 book, *The Land Where the Blues Began*, won several literary awards.

Lomax spent the last twenty years of his life working on an interactive multimedia educational computer project he called the "Global Jukebox," which included thousands of hours of sound recordings, film, videotapes and photographs. At this writing, much of this has been accomplished except for his work with the Library of Congress between 1933 and 1942, which is available only in the library archives. Getting on in years, Alan retired to Sarasota, Florida, where he lived until he passed away on July 19, 2002, at the age of eighty-seven.

Zora Neale Hurston recording Gabriel Brown and Rochelle French for the WPA in 1935. *Library of Congress. Public Domain. Image No. FA0514. State Archives of Florida,* Florida Memory, *http://floridamemory.com/items/show/107444.*

Lomax's love for diversity in people and their music sparked a modern revival in American folk music that continues to this day. He hated "commercial music" and the homogenization that the corporate recording industry imposed on modern recorded music. He felt that his work not only represented the preservation of unique and diverse creativity but also held the keys with which an evolving humanity could unlock its past.

Alton C. Morris

Florida's greatest collector of early folk songs was Alton C. Morris. Mr. Morris was born near Lake Okeechobee and, in the 1930s, began his career in musicology at the University of Florida as a field worker for the Folklife section of the WPA. Working as an intern with Alan Lomax, Stetson Kennedy and Zora Neale Hurston, he later wrote his dissertation on Florida folk songs while completing his graduate work at the University of North

Alton C. Morris, Florida musicologist and one of the founders of the Florida Folk Festival, 1958. *Robert Leahey, photographer. Image No. FP851518. Used with permission. State Archives of Florida,* Florida Memory, *http://floridamemory.com/items/show/115917.*

Carolina–Chapel Hill. In 1950, he published his work as *Folk songs of Florida*, which is still the only known collection of such songs.

Morris worked at the University of Florida for many years, teaching folklore and history classes. From 1936 until 1966, he also served as editor of the *Southern Folklore Quarterly*, and it was Morris who is credited with suggesting to the Florida Women's Music Club to create a Florida Folk Festival. When the festival was born in the 1950s, Morris was there, playing an influential role, teaching, giving lectures and even singing songs (he particularly loved "Barbara Allen") until he passed away in 1979. He was posthumously awarded the Florida folk heritage award in 1988.

THE MUSIC OF WORLD WAR II

During World War II, few states were directly affected as much as Florida. Over a quarter of a million Floridians either volunteered or were drafted into the military, and dozens of military bases were established or expanded throughout the state. German U-boats roamed the Florida coast, sinking over forty merchant ships in the Atlantic and in the Gulf. The cry "Lights out!" was often heard along the coast to keep German submarine periscopes from observing Allied ships at night. Amazingly, not a word was reported in the papers when four Nazi saboteurs landed on Ponte Vedra Beach in 1942 and, after burying their weapons and ammunition in the sand, made their way up along the beach and into Jacksonville. Another Nazi landing party had also landed in New York, and when one of the Germans there revealed their plans to the FBI, all the Nazis, including the ones waiting in Florida, were rounded up and quickly executed.

Besides men and other resources, agriculture was Florida's primary economic contribution to the war effort, but these years spurred Florida's economic development and led to a postwar population boom, a turning point in Florida's rapid growth that changed the Sunshine State forever.

By 1940, almost 80 percent of American households had radios. While World War II raged, American swing and jazz was popular throughout the world, although Hitler reminded Germans that being pro–western music was decadent. Because of their roots in black music, Hitler banned all American forms of music from occupied Europe.

One day during the war in the Pacific, a young airman took his usual spot as tail gunner on a B-25 and flew off to do his daily bombing raid.

Unfortunately on this day, the bomber was racked with Japanese Zero gunfire and shot down. The young man and the rest of his crew survived by parachuting out, but they landed far behind enemy lines and were captured by the Japanese. The young man was held prisoner for eighteen months, sometimes being placed in a small cage made of bamboo and securely tied with rope. The young man couldn't stand being held in such a small box, and he began to gnaw at the bamboo. Amazingly, he chewed his way through, wreaking havoc on his mouth, teeth and gums. When he finally managed to escape, the young man ran and hid in the jungle until he was spotted by some of the natives. Fortunately for the young aviator, they were sympathetic, and using a radio, the natives contacted a nearby U.S. destroyer, which came to retrieve the downed airman.

Years later he would tell a friend, "I was so happy to get home that when I got back to the United States I bowed down and kissed the earth." The young man's name was Will McLean.

PART TWO · TRADITIONS

5

Will McLean, the Father of Florida Folk Music

Will McLean is recognized today as the Father of Florida Folk Music. He was the first to sing it, and he encouraged everyone else to sing it as well. More than any other person, he is the reason there is a Florida folk scene at all.

Born in Chipley, Florida, in 1919, Will was a fifth-generation Floridian, a people who were friendly but kept to themselves in the back piney woods, a place where turpentine was king and times were hard. For a young boy, those back woods must have seemed like paradise. At night, the radio crackled old-time music and lightning bugs danced in the yard. Will was a typical Florida boy whose love of music was nurtured by his grandfather, who gave him his first musical instrument, a gourd and cornstalk fiddle with a horsehair bow. Even at an early age, Will showed signs of musical talent, playing church hymns on a harmonica at age three.

When Will was six years old, he was running through the back woods barefooted and stepped on a rusty wire that went through his foot. The wound became infected and was treated with a home remedy of turpentine wrap and herbs. Will ran a life-threatening fever for days and was restricted to his bed for several weeks. He recalled, years later, lying there, listening to the wild geese flying overhead, making a strange "oh-ee" sound. "I wanted to fly away and go with them," he said. "Out of that I wrote my first song, 'Away O'ee,' which I refined over the years":

Will McLean, the "Black Hat Troubadour," 1978. *Thelma Boltin, photographer. Image No. FP78447. Will McLean Foundation. Used with permission. State Archives of Florida,* Florida Memory, *http://floridamemory.com/items/show/242071.*

Away O'ee, I'll go, When the sun sinks down, And the yellow moon is big and round, Away O'ee, I'll go, Away O'ee.

Away O'ee, I'll fly, When the honking geese, Are a-sailing through the frozen sky, Away O'ee I'll fly, Away O'ee.

Away O'ee, I'll sing, A lilting song for my step is light, And my heart has wing, Away O'ee, I'll sing, Away O'ee.

Away O'ee, I'll love, The earth, the sea The people, and our God above, Away O'ee, I'll love. Away O'ee.

When in my final sleep, I trust my soul
Departs into the heavens deep
For I'll have done my best
Away O'ee!

When World II broke out, Will McLean was twenty-one years old and anxious to serve his country. He enlisted in the U.S. Air Force, and after a quick few weeks of training, Will went to the Pacific, where he became tail gunner on a B-25 bombing crew. It was during this time that he was shot down and held as a POW for a reported eighteen months until he managed to escape. His good friend Frank Thomas admits Will didn't talk much about those days in the war, and he himself remained skeptical of Will's escape story from a bamboo cage using only his teeth until one day, when Frank was performing a gig in Vero Beach. Frank says he played several of Will McLean's songs that night, and afterward an old man approached him during one of his breaks. The old man said he liked Frank's music, particularly the Will McLean songs, and it reminded him of something. He said he was the captain of a USS destroyer in the Pacific during World War II, and he remembered he picked up a downed pilot named "Wilbur McLean," and then he said "he had damaged his teeth and mouth as I recall, but that wouldn't have been your Will McLain, of course. I'm sure it was somebody else." Distracted by the crowd of people and well-wishers around them, Frank says he could only watch as the old man turned and walked away. "I was stunned," Frank said. "I realized then it was all true."

Returning to the States, Will McLean came home to Florida and was just beginning to find his own voice in songwriting, trying several styles of music. "I don't think Will considered himself a folk singer until after the big folk revival of the '50s and '60s," Frank Thomas told me. "I don't even know if he had a name for it, it wasn't bluegrass or even country. He was just singing the only way he knew how."

During these early years, other musicians like Woody Guthrie, Pete Seeger and the Kingston Trio were singing folk songs about the hardships of the poor and working class. Likewise, Will's songs began to reflect the human condition, but he added another dimension to his music. Will was concerned about the rapid, unchecked growth of progress that he saw changing the landscape of the state he grew up in. The Florida he knew and loved was being lost to land developers, greedy corporations and a new influx of population that generally didn't seem to care. Sometime after the war, Will McLean realized his purpose in life: he would try to save Florida by raising awareness in people with his songs about Florida's beauty, its history and its culture. He became a conservationist, years before the term was widely used, and he would use his art and folk music to save what he could of what he saw as his dying state.

Over the years that followed, Will McLean honed his craft, and his songs began to affect and influence others. Will's primary musical talent was his voice, and he learned very quickly how to use it. His good friend Gamble Rogers once said, "You cast a song or story like you cast a spell, and an artist has to be able to cast an aura of enchantment around it. Will had that quality." A good example of that is Will's composition "My Soul Is a Hawk":

My soul is a hawk. I am but returned from the place the Indians call "Land where the wind is born." Into the quiet and lonely spaces of the upper skies I soar. The beauty of Florida below me as thermal air currents send their song through my wing feathers and I float in ever widening circles. Yellow eyes piercing in rapture. The blues and the golds, the orange and faint pinks of sunset and I see into the far, far distance, my haven, the majestic old dead tree on whose limbs I find...My soul is a hawk.

Donning his black hat and taking the persona of the "Black Hat Troubadour," Will McLean traveled about spreading the gospel of Florida through folk music, influencing a whole generation of regional musicians and artists. He even appeared at Carnegie Hall with Pete Seeger and performed at many prestigious venues over the years.

Will sought no real fame or fortune in his life and, at times, seemed to travel from pillar to post, sometimes barely able to make ends meet, sometimes living out of his car or looking for the next couch to sleep on. Like so many other folk singers of his time, Will considered himself a free spirit, living the life he chose on his own terms. Bob Patterson, a folk singer who played music with Will many times, told me, "I spent a lot of time with Will all through 1970 to '71, and he kept a little trailer in the woods, somewhere just south of Orlando. He came and went as he pleased; he was his own man."

With songs like "Wild Hog," "Osceola's Last Words" and "Lord, Hold Back the Waters (of Lake Okeechobee)," Will McLean inspired so many Floridians and paved the way for other Florida folk singers to follow. Historical songs like "Acre Foot Johnson," "Tate's Hell" and "Dade's Massacre" were sung in the spirit of oral traditions, which documented regional history and opened up a whole new type of music for folk singers throughout Florida. Before Will, almost no one was singing songs about Florida history and traditions. Things have certainly changed since then.

Back in the 1970s and '80s, Will seemed to be everywhere in Florida, playing music with almost everyone. He preferred to play in St. Augustine with Gamble Rogers or Paul Champion, but he had friends in Gainesville, Tallahassee, Jacksonville and Lake Wales, among many other locations. The stereotypical folk singer sleeping on the couch, sometimes he overstayed his welcome; other times, he would just disappear without a word. It has been said that Will was beloved as well as tolerated. "He was a chain smoker," a friend told me on Facebook. "He slept on our couch a couple of nights and then he was gone, no goodbyes. He played his songs all night; it was cool." And in the evening when the musicians turned to drink, Will's ability to hold his liquor was legendary. "I thought I was able to do pretty well with all that, but nobody could touch Will," folk singer Bob Patterson admitted. "He could drink you under the table. He was always the last man standing."

"Will had a way about him that was sometimes hard to take," Frank Thomas admitted. "When Ann and I were first married and we moved into our new place, I didn't tell Will my address for a long time because I knew he was going to show up, looking for someone to drink with and play music for hours and hours. Being a newlywed and all, this was not what I considered a good idea." He smiled and closed his eyes for a moment. "But oh, my God, what a voice he had…" Frank's voice trailed off, remembering.

Some folks didn't like Will McLean initially, sometimes mistaking him for just a drifter or a drunk, but then Will would pick up his guitar, and with his quiet, unassuming manner, his storytelling and that powerful low voice, he would simply blow you away. "After he touched your soul," Bob Patterson suggested, "it was hard not to love the man."

Although Will wrote many wonderful songs, he rarely put them to music himself, leaving melodic responsibilities to his good friends Paul Champion, Gamble Rogers and others. Dash Moore, a well-known St. Augustine street musician who befriended Will, is credited with writing the melody to "Lord, Hold Back the Waters." "You can tell a Will McLean song," Frank Thomas suggested. "It's a bit more fanciful, more sophisticated than his usual three-or-four-chord material, which is mostly Paul Champion writing it. 'Dance of the Sandhill Crane' is a Will song, for example, it's more like a ballet than a folk song."

McLean lived his life like a Zen master, claiming almost no possessions, generously giving away to others whatever he had so that nothing and no one would tie him down. Once, he simply gave away a prized guitar given to him by folk singer Burl Ives. "I cannot possess anything I would not give up freely," he explained.

What Will did possess was a love for Florida and his memories as a child. "Back then," he said, "in the '20s, '30s and '40s, you could pull up anywhere by a stream, and you could drink the water. You should have seen Florida then. It was primitive, and it was beautiful. Trees, yellow pine trees this big around. Not like today."

Will never married, as far as we know, but he did have some relationships. Larry Mangum, one of Florida's finest folk singers and songwriters today, was a friend of Will's in his final years and does a song called "The Ghost of Will McLean," which includes these lyrics:

One night I met a woman in St. Augustine,
At a bar down on old St. George street,
Her face was familiar but I could not remember,
If I knew her, I'd forgotten her name.
She sat there and quietly listened,
As I told my musical tales,
But what I had to say seemed unimportant when I took my musical break
She said, "It's not just your music that interests me
I've been with musicians before,
But you're carrying on for the ones who've moved on,
And can't play their music anymore."

By her table I saw an old picture frame,
With a most unusual display,
Not a picture but an old sailor's watch cap,
She said it'd once belonged to Will McLean.
Well, I asked her how she came to possess it,
She said, "Will was a good friend of mine,
He depended on friends for a place to lay down
When the headlights seemed less than kind."

Now the ghost of Will McLean walks in old St. Augustine
He's just looking for some place to pick,
But he never walks alone, he's with those who've gone on,
He's with Gamble, Don Grooms and Bobby Hicks.

Will McLean referred to himself as a "simple man," but sometimes simple, unassuming men become vessels of light and influence for others. Most everyone who knew Will McLean agrees that he had that light and influence. People who met Will realized quickly that they were in the presence of someone special, someone with a talent and a spiritual awareness that they didn't see every day. In many ways, Will was right, he was just an ordinary man, but in other ways he was exceptional, and most people could sense that about him fairly quickly. Less a folk singer than a poet, Will was an exceptional artist to everyone who knew him.

In 1989, Will McLean was the recipient of the prestigious Florida Folk Heritage award, and his friend and fellow folk singer Pete Seeger described Will McLean as "the greatest living songwriter in America today." Seeger and McLean had shared several stages over the years (including Carnegie Hall), and the two remained friends all through their lives.

Near the end of his days, one of Will's hopes was to do a grand ballet about Florida, and indeed he had already written several songs for it, including "Dance of the Sandhill Cranes," but the project was never realized. Stricken with cancer, Will McLean died on January 17, 1990. He was cremated, and his ashes were spread along the banks of the Ocklawaha River. There is a permanent marker placed for Will's memory at Gore's Landing.

Dale Crider tells us it is a day he will never forget. "Will was such a dear friend. 'Hold Back the Waters' was the song that started my whole career in writing about the environment. I remember Will was singing that song on stage at the Florida Folk Festival, and I thought to myself, 'I want to do that!'" Both Dale and Don Grooms were honored to disperse Will McLean's ashes into the Ocklawaha River. Dale recalls how his friend's last wishes coincided so well with his ongoing desire to return to the "land where the wind is born": "I envisioned that night there were herons and egrets that caught minnows that had Will's ashes in them and flew him up to the tree tops and roosted him that night, and actually his soul would have been transferred to something like a hawk."

On January 24, 1990, friends of McLean performed in his honor at the Thomas Center in Gainesville. Will McLean was inducted into the Florida Artists Hall of Fame on April 17, 1996.

Today, Will's legacy continues through the Will McLean Foundation, a nonprofit organization that was created just before Will's death. Overseen by Will's good friend and confidante Margaret Longhill, she has devoted herself to keeping not only Will McLean's name and songs alive but also his goals of saving Florida through music and education, a task she has done without fail. Margaret Longhill has herself become a significant influence throughout the folk community in the last twenty-five years, and she is very much beloved and respected in the Florida folk family. Among her many duties, Margaret directs the Will McLean Folk Festival, which is held every year in the spring, usually in March. It is a wonderful three days of Florida's finest songwriters, musicians and folk singers and one of the finest folk festivals in the country.

Frank Thomas remains a member of the board of directors of the Will McLean foundation, helping to oversee the Will McLean Festival, as well as the annual Songwriting Contest in which he participates every year. "And let

Above: Collage of Margaret Longhill photos by Gail Carson. *Gail Carson Photography. Used with permission.*

Left: Will McLean looking out from the main stage at the Florida Folk Festival. *The Will McLean Foundation. Used with permission. State Archives of Florida,* Florida Memory, *http://floridamemory.com/ items/show/109920 and the Will McLean Foundation.*

me tell you something, it's not Willfest, it's the Will McLean Festival," he told me. "It's almost a sign of disrespect to call it anything but that."

Frank remembers when Will died: "He was going from the Veteran's Medical Center in Gainesville to a nursing home for rehab, so Ann and I agreed to take him in while he recovered, but he never made it."

"Will had a deep sadness about him that alcohol couldn't cover up, even though God knows he tried. He once did a song about a young boy traveling a great distance with an older man, and that was a song he wrote about himself. His grandfather kept him until he was about eight or nine or so, I believe, then he took him to his mama's, walking many miles to get there. He didn't talk about that much. He didn't talk about his war experiences too much, either; those sort of life experiences change a man."

"But I know one thing for certain," Frank Thomas leaned back in his rocker for a moment, "without Will McLean, you wouldn't be hearing all these songs about Florida today. None of this would be happening."

6

On the Shoulders of Giants We Ride:
Gamble Rogers

When your work speaks for itself, don't interrupt.
—Gamble Rogers

Gamble Rogers IV, Florida's most famous modern troubadour, was born on January 31, 1937. Raised to follow in the traditions of his father and grandfather before him, both prominent architects, Gamble chose instead the path of a folk musician when he went to New York and got involved, quite accidently, in the exploding folk scene there.

The story usually goes that Gamble happened to go along with a friend to a Serendipity Singers audition in New York and, disgusted by the apathy of the musicians who showed up, grabbed a guitar and "showed them how to do it."

Maggie Rogers, Gamble's first wife, has another spin on this old story. "In 1965, Gamble was on his way to Boston to start work at the Boston Seven Architectural Firm," she states. "The children and I were to join him as soon as they got out of school. He stopped in New York City to see an old school friend of mine, Tony Perry, whose brother John Bennett Perry (father of Matt Perry of the TV show *Friends*) was already in the Serendipity Singers. Tony has a great voice but did not play an instrument, so he asked Gamble to back him up while he auditioned. The Serendipity Singers obviously liked what they heard and offered both of them a job. That was it—no Boston Seven Architectural Firm!" she told us.

After two years or so of playing "Don't Let the Rain Come Down (Crooked Little Man)," the group's biggest hit (which rose to number six on the Billboard

Left: Gamble Rogers at the 1985 Florida Folk Festival. Peggy A. Bulger, photographer. Image No. FS85889. *Used with permission. State Archives of Florida,* Florida Memory, *http://floridamemory. com/items/ show/122017.*

Below: Gamble Rogers, Elizabeth Corrigon, Bob Patterson and Paul Champion at the South Florida Folk Festival. *From the collection of Bob Higginbotham and Paul Champion.net. Used with permission.*

Top 100 in May 1964), as well as their follow-up hit, "Beans in My Ears," (which hit number thirty on the Hot 100 a few months later), there is no indication of how Gamble felt about his experiences with the Serendipity Singers, but by 1966, he had had enough and set out on a solo career.

Gamble's act, shaped and honed over time, was difficult to describe. It was clearly a loose collection of songs and stories, all punctuated with a fingerpicking style reminiscence of Earl Scruggs, Chet Atkins and Josh White, a technique Gamble himself called "West Kentucky Choke Style." When he was on stage, he was in his element and in command, telling tall tales filled with unforgettable Florida characters all living in an imaginary county in Florida, much in the tradition of William Faulkner.

In fact, years before, William Faulkner had been Gamble's teacher for a while at the University of Virginia and no doubt a significant influence on the young man. Gamble tells how he first met the literary giant and how Gamble was at first uncharacteristically flustered and unable to speak. Faulkner barely noticed him until he looked up from his copy of *As I Lay Dying* long enough to acknowledge Gamble just for the moment. "You know, I used to be able to write…" Faulkner muttered and returned to his book. Eventually, Faulkner and Gamble did talk. One day, the great writer asked Gamble what he wanted to do with his life. Gamble hesitated, and before he could say anything, Faulkner smiled and told him, "Well then, do that!"

"I met Gamble in January of 1967 at the Tradewinds," folk singer Bob Patterson told me during an interview recently in St. Augustine. "The Tradewinds in St. Augustine was the center of the folk universe then," he said. "Around 1970–71, somewhere in there, we were doing shows with Gamble, Paul Champion, Jim Ballew, myself and Elizabeth Corrigan…" Bob hesitated as if remembering something from long ago. "You know, Liz was Gamble's first and only true on-stage partner."

Elizabeth Corrigan had already made a name for herself through TV and radio voices overs ("Smile! You're on Candid Camera!"), as well as several well-known TV commercials. "She always ended her set with a medley of her most famous commercials," Bob said. "During their time together, she looked after Gamble, and she did have an amazing voice."

In Florida, Gamble's fans and family still tell "Gamble stories" to this day. An example is this story, as told by Red Henry:

> One summer Sunday afternoon, Gamble and Liz were driving through Georgia on the way to their next gig, along a two-lane highway in South Georgia. There was plenty of traffic. They were in the Great American

Ford—Gamble's old Mustang—and it was HOT. The Great American Ford didn't have any air conditioning, so they rolled all the windows down for some air. But the trouble was that Gamble's hair, right then in 1972 or so, was about as long as it ever got, and it was blowing into his eyes. He was dodging back and forth and shaking his head to try to see. Liz said, "Gamble, let me put a couple of curlers in your hair to keep it out of your eyes." Gamble said, "NO!" Liz said, "Look, we can't have a wreck. Let me do this. When we stop for gas or something, I can take them out in a second." So Gamble said, "Well, okay," and she put two rollers in his hair on each side.

Now, as I mentioned, they were riding in the Great American Ford. On the outside, it just looked like a beat-up old Mustang, but Gamble had scrounged a couple of Lincoln Continental Mark III leather seats from somewhere and had them welded into the floorboard. Those seats were really soft and comfortable—you were sitting in the lap of luxury. Under the car's hood was a giant V-8 engine that Gamble personally kept tuned to the peak of perfection. Normally he was an extremely conservative driver, but if he ever wanted to go fast, that car would MOVE. So Gamble and Liz were going down this little road pretty fast, and there was heavy traffic in both directions. Gamble looked over on the right side of the road and noticed a whole family sitting on their front porch, enjoying Sunday afternoon: the parents, the grandparents, the children, the dogs, when suddenly—ZOOM! A driver crazily passed them on their left, with cars coming the other way and forced his way back into Gamble's lane just in time to avoid a head-on collision. Gamble was forced off the road, white-knuckling the steering wheel as he tried to control the car, fish-tailing between the trees planted along the edge of the road, tearing up the shrubbery in the yard. The whole family came off the porch and ran at him, enraged: the parents, the grandparents, the children, the dogs.

Gamble paid them no attention. He swung the car back on the road with one thing on his mind: he wanted to catch that guy and kill him. He stepped on it. Up ahead, the man pulled off into the gravel parking lot of a bar up ahead on the right side of the road. He got out of the car unsteadily and fell and then crawled on his hands and knees up to the bar door. He began banging on it and shouting, "I need a drink! Gimme a drink!" Well, it was Sunday afternoon in South Georgia, and he wasn't going to get a drink, but he didn't know that. He just kept pounding on the door.

Gamble pulled up behind him and skidded to a stop. As it happened, he had been doing some repair work on one of his guitars, and the guitar neck was lying there in the back seat. It was a hard maple neck. It had *a good hand-stop just below the peghead, which made it easy to swing like a club. The heel of the neck was a wedge-shaped piece of hard-rock maple, just right for bashing somebody's skull in! So he grabbed that guitar neck and stormed out of the car, looming up behind the drunk with his club raised, ready to smite his enemy. The man was still on the ground, clawing at the bar door and saying, "Please! Lemme in! Lemme in!"*

When the man felt Gamble's shadow fall across him, he turned and looked up. An expression of abject terror came across his face, and he whimpered, "Please, mister! Don't kill me!"

"It was at that moment," Gamble told Red later, "that I had a blinding flash of self-awareness, and I could suddenly see myself, my hair in disarray, all up in curlers, holding that guitar neck as a club, enraged and ready to kill this commode-hugging drunk. Fortunately, I did not kill him. But that flash of insight I experienced at that moment was memorable, to say the least."

Around that time, Molly Reynolds Gilmer was married to Gamble's bass player, Don Smith, who was affectionately known as the "Ace of Bass." Molly tells us:

Back in the early '70s, my then-husband and I traveled to the Grove to visit Gamble and Liz. We went to the Flick several nights, but the first visit there was memorable to me. Gamble and I happened to be out back, getting some fresh air (and the ability to hear each other) when this car pulls up to the side of the club. A friend of Gamble's got out of the vehicle with his guitar and asked Gamble for an opinion on a song he had just finished. Gamble introduced me to his friend Steve, who said he'd been working on this song for several years! However, it just wasn't coming to him, he said, until this very night! Steve played the song and my jaw dropped. I thought it was simply one of the best songs I had ever heard! Gamble listened carefully, and when Steve was finished, Gamble hesitated and finally said, "Steve, I think you got something there!" Steve was Steve Goodman, and we were the first to hear "City of New Orleans"! The song, of course, became a staple for Arlo Guthrie, and I have never forgotten that night. I'll never forget how much respect and admiration Gamble showed Steve.

After Elizabeth left the duo for greener pastures, Gamble usually played solo or with his good friends Don Smith on bass and Paul Champion on banjo and guitar. Sometimes he'd play with Bob Patterson or his old friend

Gamble at home. *Courtesy of the Rogers family. Used with permission.*

Will McLean, but he also included others from time to time. He hooked up with a young Alabama folk singer, Jimmy Buffett, for a while, showing Jimmy his tricks of the trade as they sped down Florida dirt roads together, sharing gigs. Buffett suggests much of what he learned as a showman was from Gamble. In the liner notes of his album *Fruitcakes*, Jimmy Buffett dedicated the recording to Rogers's memory and wrote that Rogers "taught me how to move an audience with dialogue and delivery as much as with music."

Over time, while he perfected his unique picking style, Gamble wrote songs that some critics have likened to the artistic levels of Mark Twain and Will Rogers, as well as his old professor William Faulkner. A recurring theme in Rogers's songs and stories are the characters and places in the fictional Oklawaha County, Florida. He recorded several LPs, including *The Lord Gives Me Grace and the Devil Gives Me Style* (1977) and *Oklawaha County Laissez-Faire* (1996) among others, on Flying Fish Records.

Michael Gordon Akers, a friend of Gambles, noted that "an interesting aspect of Gamble's work was that his genius was fed by the audience reaction. While the studio recordings showed some of that genius, getting the full flash grenade effect needed the live feel. Being there and witnessing it firsthand doesn't even have an allegorical equivalent. I was present the night he performed the song 'Honey Dipper' for the first time and never saw an audience reaction to equal it."

The Gamble Rogers Foundation has promised to release a collection of some of Gamble's most famous stories and songs, but to date there has been no such anthology. The closest thing so far is probably the DVD Gamble recorded in Tallahassee at the WFSU-TV Studios on August 16, 1984. *Gamble Roger's Homegrown Philosophy (Vol. 1)* comes closest to capturing a hint of Gamble's genius at work. Amazingly, the original tape for this program was thrown into the trash, and folk singer Doug Gauss, a good friend of Gamble's and a great admirer of his music, was fortunate enough to discover that the TV studio was purging itself of old analog recorded tapes, and he literally went "dumpster diving" to recover this video treasure.

Gamble's best live shows were at his home base at the Tradewinds Café in St. Augustine, and there he would spin his magic, night after night. Other musicians would sit in the dark, awed by Gamble's technique, and some began to try and copy Gamble's unique guitar playing. People like Charley Simmons, Jim Carrick and others hung out, paying close attention to Gamble's every riff and nuance. Charley Simmons usually introduces his own "Song for Gamble" by relating how he would go to the Tradewinds and study Gamble's technique and then go home to try out what he had learned. "I did that for two years," Charley smiles, "and then one day Gamble told me, 'Don't think I don't know what you're doing, stealing my licks!' Then Gamble laughed and said, 'Hell, I would have shown them to you, all you had to do was ask.'" There have been many tribute songs written for Gamble, but in our opinion Charley Simmons's "Song for Gamble (When Gamble Played that Old Guitar)" is hands down the best.

Those close to Gamble will tell you that the only thing bigger than Gamble's talent was his heart. Red Henry's son Chris, now an amazing bluegrass musician and performer in his own right, remembers: "We went to visit Gamble in St. Augustine when I was about 10, around 1991 or so. I wish I remembered more details, but Gamble took me and Dad out in a canoe on the water behind their house that night. It was the first time I had ever been in a canoe, and the moon was out, and it was the kind of gracious energetic extension that, to me, really is at the core of all of my memories and interactions with Gamble. He didn't have to take the time to do that, or do it so well, but he did, and that left a wonderful memory in my heart."

Gamble Rogers and granddaughter Neely Ann in St. Augustine. *Courtesy of the Rogers family. Used with permission.*

A well-known story is when Gamble had just came off a long tour from the road and, after meeting with his manager, Charles Steadham, was anxious to get home and get some much-needed rest. A man approached Gamble in the parking lot, and after a private conversation, Gamble left, following the man in his car. It turns out the man's wife was a big fan of Gamble's, but she was sick with cancer at home. Gamble followed the man to his house and put on an impromptu concert right there at her bedside, just for the two of them.

Gamble had many people who loved him and called him friend. "He was famous in many circles," Bob Patterson told me, "but whenever he went to a party or gathering, he always greeted the children and animals first. I loved that about the man."

Gamble's friend Jim Carrick remembers: "I met Gamble Rogers in about 1976, I think. A friend of mine called and said there was a really good finger picker playing that day in Fernandina Beach. We drove up and—man! I had never seen anything like it up close. I spoke with him after the show and met the most personable, generous and articulate man I have ever known. That day changed everything. I left for Nashville shortly after that but kept in touch with Gamble until about 1980, when I came home to Florida and moved to St Augustine to sit at his feet.

"St Augustine was a magical place in those days," Jim continued. "Music was everywhere. Gamble would always make time to show me some licks when he was home. Many times, he would talk me through what I was working on over the phone. Gamble introduced me to the Merle Travis style of finger picking. He also taught me the Joe Pass style of playing chords and embellishments. I learned from him to let the guitar tell part of the story and not be just an accompaniment. We became good, lifelong friends. When Gamble died, the whole town was devastated. I remember him saying, 'Folk music is like a river. It retreats underground only to return to the surface after a time.' I'll always remember him, and I check that river every day."

Gamble was a regular at the Florida Folk Festival for many years and held a regular jam there called the "Liar's Workshop." Like old-timers telling fishing tales, the more exaggerated the embellishment, the better the song was received. In May 1991, Gamble played the Florida Folk Festival as he had done so many times before, and although folks didn't realize it, it was the last time he would ever perform there. "I remember it was one of those wet, rainy weekends at the festival," John Alison told me. "Looking back on it now, I believe the sky was crying." Ironically, Gamble's last performance at the Florida Folk Festival (with Don Grooms, Dennis Devine and Landon Walker on bass) was actually a tribute to his old friend Will McLean, who had died the year before.

There are times in your life when you get bad news, and the moment becomes so crystallized that you remember forever where you were and what you were doing. Late in the evening of October 10, 1991, phones began to ring all over the state and beyond, a network of folk musicians and fans, young and old, hundreds and hundreds of people who got the call that day or the next. Some people remember hearing it first on NPR. "I was stunned," was the general consensus. Some people broke down and wept when they heard. "We've lost Gamble!" "It was so unreal" and "so unbelievable," many recalled. He was just fifty-four years old! How did this happen?

The news is well-known history now. Gamble died a hero's death, trying to rescue a drowning Canadian tourist, forty-eight-year-old Raymond J. Tracey, at Flagler's Beach, where Tracey had been surf fishing most of the day. Both men perished, pulled under by the ocean's rough sea and significant riptide.

Syd Ansbaucher was with Gamble that day. Syd was Gamble's friend and his attorney, and the two men, along with their wives, had spent a nice day bicycling and visiting some of Gamble's favorite sites around that area. Syd was a Jacksonville lawyer, representing Gamble and a few of his neighbors in a legal battle involving a nearby landowner who wanted to put a long dock out into the river they all used, in essence blocking it off to boaters. "After a year or so of legal wrangling, we were ready to meet with the judge that Monday for a possible decision. Gamble was in a good mood," Syd told us. "It was a beautiful day," Syd offered and then hesitated sadly, "except for the ending."

We had just eaten at the Snack Shack, and we rode down to the beach where we were camping out that night. Gamble and I had been trading books back and forth, and he had turned me on to Louis L'Amour. He and our wives were getting things ready for camp, and I went up to the public bathrooms and I took my paperback with me. The last thing Gamble told me was "Enjoy the book." I didn't think anything of it, really. I read a little bit of it when I was in there, and by the time I got out, Gamble was already gone. It all happened so quickly. My wife almost drowned going into the surf to rescue him, and she ended up in the hospital a few days after that.

"You know, years earlier I had worked as a lifeguard, and the irony of that wasn't lost on me," Syd mentioned, "although frankly the riptide was so bad, I'm not sure there was anything I could have done." Both the Canadian tourist and Gamble died in the surf that day. It was a tragedy that should have never happened, but it did. Sadly, as hard as it was to believe, Gamble was gone. "I remember Gamble had invited me over that day to tag along," his friend and folk singer Dale Crider told me, almost on the verge of tears even now. "I passed it off, thinking there would always be another time."

Today, Gamble's legacy and memory live on, not only in the hearts of those who loved him and knew how special he really was but also in those of all the musicians and artists and just regular folks whose lives he touched. Gamble Rogers influenced every musician and performer who ever crossed his path, and for some, he changed their lives significantly and forever, turning their whole way of making music around. More than any other person, Gamble Rogers was the living embodiment of Florida folk music.

In honor of his heroism, the Florida legislature renamed the state park where Gamble drowned as the Gamble Rogers Memorial State Recreation Area at Flagler Beach. Gamble is a recipient of the Florida Folk Heritage Award, and the Gamble Rogers School in St. Augustine is named in his

Stone monument at Gamble Rogers State Park. *Courtesy of author.*

Sign for Gamble Rogers Middle School in south St. Augustine. *Courtesy of author.*

Gamble Rogers entertaining his granddaughter at their home in St. Augustine. *Courtesy of the Rogers family. Used with permission.*

honor. There is also a Gamble Rogers Middle School down U.S. 1 in the south part of St. Augustine. Every year, during the first weekend in May, the Gamble Rogers Folk Festival is held in the Oldest City.

Red Henry remembers, "Christopher and I drove down from Virginia for Gamble's services. Gamble's wife, Nancy, kindly invited us, together with my mother, Renee, to the private morning service, and then we also attended the much larger afternoon service at the lighthouse. There was some picking afterward with friends, but Chris and I had to eventually start back home. I remember Liz Corrigan was there as well," he said. "I heard she passed away soon after that. My heart goes out to Charlie Robertson for taking on the job of hosting the afternoon event and carrying it out with dignity and his characteristic aplomb."

Finally, in regards to Gamble Rogers's ability to embellish and tell a good yarn, Gamble's first wife, Maggie, sends the following note along:

As far as all the little details and facts about Gamble, I am not sure that it even matters what the exact truth is. Gamble was always an embellisher, so I suppose it's appropriate that stories about him are as well. Whatever, he was a remarkable man, who had a great drive and a great discipline that few people ever got to see the workings of, just the end results. He worked hard to be good, and fortunately in his life he had some wonderful influences, just to mention a couple, his father and my uncle Jack. Please thank all your readers for the attention they have given Gamble, and thanks for remembering him.

Gamble is missed most of all by his own family, of course. His granddaughter Neely Ann (Miller) still refers to her grandfather as her hero, and through his encouragement as a young girl, she cherished reading for him and hearing him tell her how much he was delighted with her progress in school. She would often sit at his feet while he worked, sometimes watching as he played the guitar, and whenever he played "Puff the Magic Dragon," she knew it was just for her. Neely had just turned nine years old when her grandfather died, and many years later, she wrote the following:

I wish so much to be that little girl again, running down Little Beach and wearing my grandpa's floppy hat over my eyes. Those days will be treasured forever. When we walked in the soft marsh sand, it would make huge footprints and I would follow him, stepping in my grandpa's muddy impressions, jumping from one footprint to the next. Now, he is gone and I have no more footprints to follow because they were washed away, leaving me with only the memories to hold onto.

Gamble Rogers's skill, his talent and his genius remain undisputable. He is remembered as a kind and generous soul who always took time to make a personal connection with almost everyone he met. Today, his legacy is alive in the Florida folk community and beyond. Gamble Rogers is and will be remembered, without question, as Florida's greatest folk singer.

"Cousin" Thelma Boltin and the Florida Folk Festival

B orn in Beaufort, South Carolina, on August 31, 1904, Thelma Boltin moved with her family to Gainesville, Florida, in 1907. After attending Gainesville's public schools, Thelma journeyed north to study drama at Emerson College in Boston before returning to teach at Gainesville High School, where she also became the state's first certified high school speech teacher. Thelma Boltin was the city's first recreational director, Children's Creative Theater director and a founding member of the Gainesville Little Theater. She was known regionally because of her storytelling gifts and was featured on the *Story Lady Hour* over WGGG radio. She also participated in the Florida State Museum's annual Heritage Fair and Collectors Day on the UF campus and was director of the Gainesville Community Center prior to 1954, when she was appointed director and overseer of the Florida Folk Festival.

Succeeding Sarah Gertrude Knott as director of the Florida Folk Festival, Thelma Boltin became directly involved in recruiting talent, scouting the state for folk artists and sometimes holding auditions over the telephone, sometimes traveling a long distance to see an artist or folk act. With the valuable assistance of Barbara Beauchamp, Thelma took the Florida Folk Festival and turned it into a valuable statewide institution for sharing and celebrating Florida's history and traditions.

Johnny Bullard, a member of the singing Bullard family, as well as a White Springs historian and council member, related a bit of Florida Folk Festival history in a recent interview: "I first attended the festival in 1969, when I performed with some of my schoolmates," he recalls. "We

Fletcher Hodges Jr., Sarah G. Knott, Thelma Boltin and Alton C. Morris, founding members of the Florida Folk Festival, 1960. *Image No. FA3881. Used with permission. State Archives of Florida,* Florida Memory, *http://floridamemory.com/items/show/109804.*

were excited to be there. We had all sold programs to get a chance to participate." He continues:

> *Without Stephen Foster's "Old Folks at Home," there would probably be no Florida Folk Festival. The song became the official state song of Florida in 1935, and soon afterwards, it was decided that Florida needed a memorial to Stephen Foster and his most famous song. Eli Lilly, the pharmaceutical king from Indianapolis, Indiana, had a large collection of Stephen Foster memorabilia, and he came down here where he got on a boat with Ms. W.A. Saunders and other civic leaders and decided White Springs was the place. One hundred acres were received from three or four Florida Federation of Music Clubs, and then title was transferred to the Stephen Foster Memorial Commission, which was an independent agency that answered only to the governor.*

Program for the 1955
Florida Folk Festival.
Florida Memory, *Florida
State Archives. Used
with permission. http://
www.floridamemory.com/
collections/folklife/festival_
programs.php?year=1955.*

When it was decided to create a music festival at the park, a meeting was held in 1952 at the Colonial Hotel to decide what kind of music would be played. Folk music was the obvious choice, and they contacted Mrs. Sarah Gertrude Knot, from FDR's New Deal WPA Program, to promote the folk festival. In 1953 and 1954, Ms. Knot was the main director and emcee. Thelma Boltin from Gainesville was an obvious choice to assist, and she and Ms. Saunders went all over the state to invite "folk groups" of all kinds to come and perform. They tried to find as many diverse groups as they could and did a pretty good job. Those first festivals included Minorcans from St. Augustine, Cubans from Ybor City and Miami, Seminoles from the Everglades and even some African Americans, which they caught some flak over, as it was unheard of back then.

Ms. Knot retired from the commission after the second festival in 1954, and Thelma Boltin took it over after that. Ms. Thelma ran a tight ship,

"Cousin" Thelma Boltin, supreme director of the Florida Folk Festival for over twenty-five years, beginning in 1955. *Karl E. Holland, photographer. Image No. CO32861. 1960. Used with permission. State Archives of Florida*, Florida Memory, *http:// floridamemory.com/items/ show/77516.*

and she had some rules that you had to abide by if you wanted to play there. Females had to wear skirts, support undergarments, shoes that covered top of feet, while the men had to wear collared shirts tucked in with a belt. If you got on stage and she disapproved of what she saw or what you were doing, she wouldn't hesitate, she'd interrupt the act, saying, "Let's clap them off the stage!"

Ken Crawford, a friend and a folk singer who's been around quite a while, tells us the following story:

Once upon a time in the late '70s, I was with a group of players and singers from Stuart/Jensen Beach, Florida. We called ourselves the Back Porch Band at that time, since that's where we practiced (no relation to past or current back porch or front porch ensembles). We were playing the Florida Folk Festival in White Springs, and it was about 9:30 p.m. or so on Saturday night at the Main Stage/Amphitheater. We had just finished a song about the festival that we wrote in the campground that morning, called "A Gathering in the Live Oaks," followed by our spirited rendition of the sea chantey "Poor Ol' Rubin Ramsail" when the crowd stood and applauded (at least the front row, I couldn't see the rest of them out there in the dark). That's when I saw a few people lighting matches and lighters too, and for a moment it began to feel like a Melanie concert, truly a heady experience from my point of view on this side of the monitors. In these few seconds, when I should have been paying attention to the set time left onstage, it was the applause, the general vibration of the evening, the growing smiles on the faces of my bandmates, and a great surge of misplaced confidence, that gave birth to an idea, then a question, which I spoke loudly and directly into the microphone as I turned, beaming, in the direction of the stage emcee standing quiet and powerful at the podium behind me. "Can we do one more song? How about one more?!" Seconds passed, then seconds more that seemed like minutes, and still only silence coming from the stout figure dressed all in white looming there at the side of the stage. The crowd was silenced by it, and my bandmates were confused by it. We looked each other over, dumbfounded, as we wondered what had happened to our happy little reception there on the stage. Then, at the precise moment we thought it could go on no longer, the specter presiding over us (this had suddenly become very apparent) spoke: "NO—YOU CAIN'T! TIMES UP—AND THAT'S IT!" she said. Reeling from this response, delivered with power and sheer truth, and with the correctness of those words echoing in my head, I turned back round to look at the audience, incredulous. My mind sought something else to concentrate upon, and I became fascinated all at once by small things that were going on around me. It was then that the match-holders in front of me bent down, and I realized suddenly that someone had only lost their keys and that people standing next to them were just helping to find them. This only added insult to injury. As the moment fell around us like broken glass, we waved limply at the audience, smiled weakly, and tried not to look completely crushed as we quietly slid off into the night. We, of course, had just experienced the well-known wrath of Cousin Thelma Boltin. In fact, we had been rightly "Thelma-ized," learning our lesson once and for all about the academic subject called Stage Ethics 101.

It was obviously a lesson well learned, because Ken Crawford later went on to become director of the Florida Folk Festival himself in later years, from 1995 to 2000.

Tower at Stephen Foster State Park at sunset, White Springs, Florida. *Robert Leahey, photographer. Image No. FT13813A. Used with permission. State Archives of Florida,* Florida Memory, *http://floridamemory.com/items/show/124245.*

Johnny Bullard reminds us, "We didn't refer to her as 'Cousin' Thelma, out of respect, that was just her stage name. We called her Miss Thelma or Miss Boltin." Johnny told us earlier of an incident that happened the first time "Diamond Teeth" Mary took the stage at the festival. Thelma didn't approve of Mary and found the diamonds embedded in her front teeth too much to take. A mutual friend suggested to Mary that she open up her performance that afternoon with "Amazing Grace," which was Miss Boltin's favorite. Being the good entertainer that she was, Diamond Teeth Mary did just that, earning her Miss Boltin's instant admiration, as well as a regular spot on the festival for the next several years. "You had to know how to work with Miss Boltin," Johnny suggested, "or she wouldn't have you back."

For years, Ms. Boltin was the mistress of ceremonies along with her trusted assistant Barbara Beauchamp, both of whom were later awarded the Florida Folk Heritage Award. Together they ran the show until 1976, when the Florida Folk Life Program and the first staff folklorists took over. Thelma became less and less involved after that until she retired.

By that time, with the onset of the newer, more independent and sometimes rebellious artists, including Will McLean, Gamble Rogers and Don Grooms, as well as advancement in age, Cousin Thelma begun to loosen her firm grip of control over the festival. In her final years there, Barbara Beauchamp took over most of the paperwork and administrative duties, while Thelma oversaw emcee duties at the festival.

THE "GREAT HIPPIE INVASION" OF 1972

In 1970 and 1971, the festival planners at the Florida Folk Festival began to notice a peculiar thing. The marketing for FFF had been unusually successful in its advertising and getting the word out through the usual channels, e.g. newspapers, TV ads, etc., but a new wrinkle had been added. The new long-playing-album-format FM radio stations had attracted a large and loyal audience base, especially in college towns such as Gainesville and Tallahassee, as well as at colleges outside the state. All this was on the heels of Woodstock in 1969 and several large festivals in Atlanta, and festivals were now very cool in some circles. For a while, Mrs. Boltin and her staff seemed delighted to see their little festival growing into a bigger national event. What they hadn't reckoned on was the "Great Hippie Invasion of 1972." Even today, veteran Florida Folk Festival goers may close their eyes and shake their heads, and indeed, some refuse to talk about it. As if they had survived some traumatic experience, some of the people who were there still wonder if it was an unreal dream that descended upon the festival, although some would describe it more as a nightmare.

Most estimates put the crowd size that year at 100,000, although estimates vary, wildly. Since the average FFF weekend brings in about 25,000 to 30,000 souls, one can see the obvious effects of a crowd that size. "I loved it," Bettina Makley recalls, "There were thousands of people; it was exciting for me. My mother [Elroyce Makley] told us to stay on the campgrounds in the park, so naturally I took my autoharp and jumped the fence to see what the fuss was all about. I was just a teenager then; all I remember that year was playing music and dancing. It was beautiful, really."

Besides the sheer number of people, the real problem, of course, was the fact that most of these people were hippies! And hippies, the 1972 White

Springs Police Department realized, meant sex, drugs and, in a word, trouble. In fact, some remember there was quite a bit of marijuana smoke in the air and that, along with an especially potent crop of psilocybin mushrooms that year from the nearby "cowchip belt," only added to the surrealistic quality of the event. Unfortunately, what was especially disconcerting to the citizenry and festival directors was the public nudity. Even Ms. Thelma Boltin had to announce from the stage: "There will be no naked swimming in the Suwannee!"

The good citizens of White Springs didn't know what to think, and although many considered it much ado about nothing, others seemed overwhelmed by it all. By the time the festival was over that year, there was already serious discussion about cancelling the festival, this time forever. Cooler heads prevailed, but the festival for next year was moved back from Memorial Day in May to Labor Day, August 31. Part of the rationalization for moving the festival date was the flood waters that ran high that year, but it seemed to everyone that the real reason was to avoid another "hippie invasion." Indeed, the festival continued to be held on Labor Day (the final weekend in August into September) from 1973 through 1976 before it was finally returned to Memorial Day weekend in 1977.

THE OLD MARBLE STAGE

In 1953 and 1954, when the festival first started, there was only one wooden stage. In 1955, the Barnett Bank in Jacksonville donated several tons of marble stone to the festival, and a new marble stage was created that was known as the main stage. Happy to donate it to a worthy cause, the Barnett Bank transferred it all over in 1955 (although curiously, the Florida Folk Festival programs from 1955 to 1958 don't mention it). In 1975, the main stage was moved to the newly constructed amphitheater, and the old stage was rechristened the "Old Marble Stage." After the Florida Folklife Program took control of the festival in 1979, it added several stages, including the Folklife Narrative Stage, the Storytelling Stage, the Heritage Stage, the Gazebo Stage, the Azalea Stage and several impromptu stages. The number and location of the many other stages varied from year to year.

For many musicians and artists who are accepted to play at the Florida Folk Festival every year, the Old Marble Stage remains the most important primarily because of its rich history and tradition. With rare exception, it

Sixth-graders from Forest Hills Elementary School in Jacksonville, Florida, performing at White Springs, circa 1960. *Image No. FA3791. Used with permission. State Archives of Florida,* Florida Memory, *http://floridamemory.com/items/show/109723.*

is usually reserved for those who have proved themselves over these many years, and getting the chance to perform on it is considered a great honor, even to this day.

After the Florida State Department established the Bureau of Florida Folklife Programs in White Springs in 1976, it coordinated the festival until 1995. At that time, the Florida Folklife Program was relocated to Tallahassee, and the general festival administration was taken over by the Museum of Florida History. In 2002, Secretary of State Katherine Harris announced they were cutting ties with the festival, and the State Department would no longer manage it. Out of money and pressed for time, there was much concern about whether there would even be a fiftieth-anniversary Florida Folk Festival.

One surprising benefactor who came through for the festival that year was the owner of the New York Yankees, George Steinbrenner, who was also a Tampa shipbuilder at that time. After he read an editorial in the

Tampa Tribune highlighting the problem, George donated $78,000 to keep the festival alive, prompting the State of Florida to follow suit with its own donation of $110,000. Very soon after that, David Struhs, secretary of the Department of Environmental Protection, announced that the Florida Parks Service, a division of the DEP, would assume the responsibility of producing the festival.

Following Ken Crawford's time as director of the FFF from 1995 to 2000, Jon Kay became the festival director (he was a noted dulcimer player himself) and stayed until 2004. More currently, Donald V. Forgione has been the Parks Service director and oversees Florida's 170-plus state parks, while Elaine McGrath has been the park and festival director. With rare exception, the festival been held every year during the Memorial Day weekend, and to date, it remains the longest continually running state-sponsored music festival in the United States.

Having retired in the 1980s from emcee work, Thelma Boltin passed away in 1992, at age eighty-eight. She never married and never had children, but she is considered by many to be the matriarch of the Florida Folk Festival. Her family and "children" are the many folk singers she came to know and introduce to state residents and festivalgoers over those many years in White Springs. She remains a legend in Florida folk history and is remembered to this day as the stern "mother" who managed to turn their little state festival into one of the finest musical events in the nation.

Paul Champion, the World's Greatest Banjo Player

Paul Champion was the bridge between Florida folk and Florida bluegrass for many years. Some bluegrass or folk musicians will tell you the two types of music are exclusive from each other and that this bears out in the separate bluegrass and folk festivals held throughout the United States today. To Paul Champion, it was all just music. Bringing home to Florida the seeds of the New York '60s folk revolution, along with bandmate Art Schill of the Folksters and Gamble Rogers who headed the Serendipity Singers, Paul met up with Will McLean, and together they ignited what became the modern-day Florida folk community.

George Paul Champion Jr. was born on March 23, 1938, to a military family stationed in the Panama Canal Zone. Both his father and uncle were colonels in the army. Paul's father was born in Illinois, but his family roots were in Kentucky, while Paul's mother was from Louisiana. In 1955, Paul was performing bluegrass and country songs with friends and fellow musicians Buzz Buzby, Vance Trull and Charlie Waller, and it was clear Paul had an enormous talent for music even then. During those years he worked with a group called the Log Cabin Boys, and played a variety of instruments, including the pedal steel guitar. Sometime around 1956 or 1957, Paul won the national amateur banjo contest, and he was determined, he told friends, to become "the greatest banjo player in the world."

In the back of Paul's mind, however, he knew he was destined to follow in his father's footsteps, and in July 1956, Paul applied for and was admitted to West Point Academy, much to the delight of his family. During the physical exam, however, the military doctors detected a heart murmur, probably due to his having rheumatic fever as a child. Paul was rejected from military service and sent home.

Paul tried to make the best of the situation. He attended Florida State University and afterward headed off to New York, where he had heard the music of Pete Seeger, Ramblin' Jack Elliot and Dave Van Ronk, among others. There he met up with fellow Floridian Art Schill of Jacksonville, who was performing with his all-Florida trio, the Folksters. The group was made up of Art on guitar, Ken Hodges on bass and Fred Williams, from St. Augustine, on guitar. Art knew about Paul's musical ability and insisted he join the group. They had just signed with Mercury Records to do their first folk album, which they called *New...In Folk*.

Paul joined the group but insisted on being his own man. The Folksters trio would all wear the same clothes, creating "a look," but Paul refused to dress the same as the others and would wear something different, usually a suit. The Folksters played many of folk music's biggest venues, including the Hungry i and the Blue Angel, and they even made an appearance on *The Tonight Show with Johnny Carson*. As a promotion idea from their record company, the foursome were all given different colored Corvettes to drive to their gigs. Unfortunately, the Folksters never had a significant hit record, and their hootenanny style of folk was just beginning to wane, so the group disbanded in 1963. Nigel and Kenny went on to create the folk group Spanky and Our Gang, and Art Schill returned home to Jacksonville, where he invested in the Saki Shop, his own folk club there. Paul came home, too, but he was already making plans to team up with the obvious genius of one of the Serendipity Singers alumni, Gamble Rogers, who had himself returned home to St. Augustine.

Paul Champion complemented Gamble's rapid-fire guitar technique so well that the two became inseparable on stage. Along with Will McLean and Bob Patterson, Paul followed Gamble to as many festivals and shows as he could. Will McLean also began performing with Paul, and in fact, it was Paul who wrote much of the music and melodies behind many of Will McLean's songs.

Paul was memorable in many ways and influenced musicians wherever he went, but remarkably, he never said a word on stage. He let his music do all his talking. Of course, usually Gamble or Will were more than happy to do vocals and talk in between songs, but Paul never uttered a word. He did, however, go down to the audience and greet his fans during breaks in the music, some of whom had driven a long way just to hear him play.

Paul Champion and Gamble Rogers at the Florida Folk Festival, 1985. *Folklife Collection. Image No. FA4515. Used with permission. State Archives of Florida,* Florida Memory, *http:// floridamemory.com/items/show/110411.*

Paul was a regular in a lot of circles, including the bluegrass shows down at the Malabar in Jacksonville, among others, with Mike Johnson. "He knew a lot of songs," Mike remembered. "He was an amazing musician. We always loved it when Paul came in to play."

If there was one thing Paul loved more than music, it was probably his musical instruments. He cherished his treasures, and treasures they were, including several Granada banjos and a beautiful Martin D-45. One famous story was how in 1963, Bob Dylan dropped Paul's Gibson flathead RB-3 banjo and broke the resonator. Paul got it fixed later, but he wasn't happy with Bob that night.

The heart ailment that Paul had all his life, which kept him out of the army, finally caught up with him, and at forty-seven years old, he died on Valentine's Day 1986 in Gainesville. At his funeral, his friend Gamble Rogers delivered the eulogy, which included these words:

> *Here was a man whose talents and abilities were so potent that he established a national reputation and a devoted and loyal following without ever being featured on a major recording label, and without ever uttering a word over a microphone while on stage. For most of his life, Paul Champion performed for a living, but it should be stated that Paul lived to perform. The passion and love that he conveyed through his music are what elevated him to an almost mythical status in his own time.*

Did Paul achieve his goal of becoming the world's best banjo player? Some would suggest that, in fact, he did. Today, Paul Champion's legacy and his influence can been seen at the many Florida folk and bluegrass festivals throughout the region. In Florida folk history, bluegrass artists like Vassar Clements, Chubby Anthony and Chubby Wise have come and gone, all making their mark, while artists such as Mike Johnson, John Hedgcoth, Red and Murphy Henry (and now their son Chris Henry), as well as the Peyton Brothers, among so many others, are all keeping the bluegrass lineage alive and well in Florida folk music circles. This cross-pollination of musical styles has everything to do with Paul Champion, and although he would never say so out loud from a stage, we think Paul would approve. It certainly worked for him.

9

Lullaby of the Rivers: Bob Patterson

B ob Patterson is an unassuming, soft-spoken man whose wry smile is both charming and disarming. His eyes are soft but clear, and in conversation, it is obvious he has a low tolerance for BS. We were at O.C. White's in St. Augustine, where he reminded me he's been playing "every Thursday evening for the past twenty years." As we chatted and ate a fine lunch, he told us about his own Florida folk history, and it is, in a word, remarkable. "The first night I rolled into town, January 1967, I was sleeping on the beach," he smiled. "I went over to the Tradewinds that evening, which I had heard was the place to go back then. I was thinking that I might get a gig or something, so I walked down with my twelve-string guitar, and there was Paul Champion and Jim Ballew playing on stage. They sounded real good, and when they had a break, we met, and they introduced me to Duke and Tony, the people who owned Tradewinds then. To make a long story short, before I ended up leaving that night, I had a gig playing for six nights a week for the next six weeks!" Bob smiled, "But wait, it gets better."

"So I played a short set and was hanging around, and then someone touches me on the shoulder and he thrusts out his hand to me. 'Hi, I'm Gamble Rogers,' he told me, and then he introduces me to his good friend, Will McLean. That was my first night in town, and that's how I got introduced to St. Augustine." Bob grins at the memory of it. "I love this town."

Bob Patterson has been playing folk music in Florida for almost half a century now, and he is one of Florida's premier performers, songwriters and spoken word storytellers. He has recently taken to writing in addition to performing his music and has authored several books, including *Forgotten*

Florida Tales, published by The History Press. It's been a long journey for Bob, but it is an adventure filled with twists, turns and unexpected delights along the way.

"I was with this psychedelic group, Elizabeth, in the late '60s," Bob recalls. "We signed with Vanguard Records, and after we got some airplay with the song 'Mary Ann,' we began playing in front of thousands of people on tour. To be honest, I wasn't really that invested in it, you know? Ironically, my most successful time in the music business happened when I could have cared less." He continued:

When we recorded that album for Vanguard, they put us up at the Chelsea Hotel where Janis Joplin and Country Joe were staying. We'd run into them all the time. I believe they had a bit of a romance going on, but I don't think it lasted much after that. We opened concerts for everybody, Janis Joplin, Country Joe and the Fish, Vanilla Fudge, Moby Grape, Blue Cheer, even Muddy Waters. We did an appearance on the Mike Douglas Show *and did a live performance from Steel Pier in Atlantic City. It was a good time, the be-ins, the love-ins, playing in front of ten thousand people, good times. Unfortunately, the music was so loud, it was deafening on stage. I was playing this twelve-string, and we had everything all turned up. Sadly, I lost a significant amount of my hearing then. Kind of ironic, thinking about how I was director of an ear, nose and throat clinic in the navy a few years before that.*

I had a little bit of royalty money from our biggest seller, "Mary Ann," and I wanted to put it to good use, so I decided to move to Florida. I drove down to St. Augustine, and I got a house behind the old Sugar Mill, big house, lots of room, forty dollars a month! Everything was cheap here back then. I got that regular gig at the Tradewinds, me and Don Smith, and whenever Gamble came into town, Don and I would back him up. We worked six, seven months out of the year that way, playing five nights a week. The other five months we'd go gigging around; there were lots of coffee houses and clubs in Gainesville and Jacksonville. So, we did OK.

I was born in Newark, New Jersey, and raised in Pontin Lakes. I had a great youth. My dad worked for GE, and we moved all over the place: East Texas, New York State, Kentucky. The only music I played when I was a kid was on the radio. What first got my attention was probably the Kingston Trio. We were listening to Jimmy Reed, but we were all singing Kingston Trio songs. I was graduating from Tyler High School in Texas and went down to Rush week at the University of Texas and was at some fraternity. I remember some guy, sitting in the middle of the room, playing folk songs, and there must've been a couple of dozen people sitting around him, singing along. It struck me, here was this guy, whoever he was, and he had that whole little audience in the palm of his hand. I was impressed, anyway. I met him later; his name was Segal Pride, and he gave me a copy of Pete Seeger's book How to Play 12 String. *I learned all those chords, one chord at a time.*

Even today, when Bob plays out live in the clubs and festivals, his main instrument continues to be the twelve-string guitar. "I've always played twelve-string. It was something different, and it separated me from the pack. I learned about Lead Belly and Blind Lemon, all these guys who played twelve-string, and I tried to learn their songs."

When Bob first met the love of his life, Joline, he began teaching her how to play the bass, and before long, she was on stage singing and playing along. Together they have traveled all over the United States, including festivals, colleges, clubs, resort hotels and premier listening rooms. They even appeared on the Nashville Star Search competition *You Can Be a Star.* Eventually, the two blended their talents to include elements of folk, country, blues, ragtime and storytelling.

When a fuller band was needed, Bob and Joline relied on Dick Kraft on flute, saxophones and banjo; Chip Herrington on harmonica; and Bill Temme on stand-up percussion, collectively known as the Friends of Mine Band.

Bob has written many great songs, but perhaps his most well-known composition is "Lullaby of the Rivers," which has won Bob much praise and many awards. The song's lyrics go as follows:

If I could only release time, oh, I'd go back a hundred years,
To a place where I could listen to the lullaby of the rivers.
For now and then there will arise, out of the waters, Indian spirits,
To tell me how they got their names, and sing the lullaby of the rivers.
Oklawaha, Ichetucknee, Econfina, Withlacoochee,
Apalachicola, Wakulla, Wacissa, Aucilla,
Caloosahatchee, Kissimmee, Ochlockonee, Choctahatchee
Econolahatchee and the Suwanee are singing the lullaby of the rivers.
If you have ears enough for listening, oh, you can hear what they are saying.
You can hear them all singing the lullaby of the rivers.
The moving water makes the music, the pureness creates the healing
The reflections give up the secrets of the lullaby of the rivers.

Left: Bob Patterson at the 1977 Florida Folk Festival. *Image No. FA4031. Used with permission. State Archives of Florida*, Florida Memory, *http://floridamemory.com/ items/show/109949.*

Below: Collage of Bob Patterson photos, all taken by Gail Carson for Gail Carson Photography. *Used with permission.*

Bob cites his old friend Gamble Rogers as his most significant influence in his music. "Gamble knew that I was totally entranced about how beautiful Florida was and told me one day that he wanted to show me one of his sacred places. A few days later, he arrived at my house in his lime green Ford Mustang towing a boat trailer with his Thompson's Runabout on board. Will McLean was in the car. We headed west out of town along two-lane blacktop roads out past Fort McCoy and down a dirt road to Gore's Landing on the Ocklawaha River." Bob paused a moment as he remembered that day:

What happened next I can only describe as an awakening of all those things I experienced growing up alongside of my own river as a child. I was in a place where nature and spirit were yearning for each other. The Ocklawaha was like nothing I could imagine, except in some Tarzan movie. I spread myself out on my belly across the bow of the boat with my old Leica camera and started taking pictures and getting lost in my bliss. For Gamble and Will, I knew they felt like it was their mission to show me this place that the poet Sidney Lanier called "the sweetest water lane in all the world." It was a gift, and I embraced it with joy and gratitude. It was no wonder to me that when Gamble created the landscape for his wonderful characters to unfold, he would call it Ocklawaha County.

Bob continued to play music with Gamble, Will and Paul Champion until they all eventually passed away. His partner Joline is currently not in the best of health and is no longer able to perform music on stage. Bob Patterson continues along as he has always done, touching the lives of others and influencing the next generation of Florida folk singers. He continues to play festivals throughout the state and beyond and is instrumental in the annual Gamble Rogers Folk Festival, held in St. Augustine, usually in the first week of May. Bob has also added his talents to the HAWKE Wildlife Association's Music for the Birds Concert for over twenty years, and he is known to include his voice to many benefits and causes that have requested his presence over these many years.

Bob recorded a DVD in 2013 in Ponte Vedra, Florida, and the recording is an excellent example of Bob's live performance, including his storytelling and his songs. The DVD is available on his website, Floridastoryteller.com.

Bob has always had a knack for telling a good story, and his stage show usually includes narratives and spoken word histories surrounding the songs he plays. Bob remains an active member of the Florida Storytelling Guild, and his book *Forgotten Florida Tales* (The History Press, 2009) continues to sell well. His most recent book, *Dorothy*, follows a young girl's adventures in North Florida, a story that includes the Great Fire of Jacksonville in 1901. He plans to follow up with a new book very soon. In 2011, Bob was the recipient of the prestigious Mother Earth and Fellow Man award, which is given by the Stetson Kennedy Foundation for individuals who have "made a difference in folklore." Also that year, Bob won another award for his song "Lullaby of the Rivers," this time for the Best Florida Song award, given by the North Florida Folk Network (NFFN) in Jacksonville.

As we finished our interview, Bob and I made our way out of the restaurant and shook hands in departure. "Bob, it's an amazing life story, I have to admit," I told him. He grinned and told me, "I guess you could say I'm a very lucky man!" I would certainly have to agree.

10

Charlie Robertson:
Our Mutual Friend

In my research for this book, it struck me that there seemed to be two actual geniuses that I had come across in the history of the Florida folk scene. One was the late Gamble Rogers, and the other was Charlie Robertson. "Charlie is the best folk singer I have ever known," Gamble Rogers was fond of saying. When you watch Charlie perform, it is easy to see why. "Charlie's been around since the old days," Bob Patterson reminded us. "He and Don Dunaway [a regular performer at St. Augustine's Milltop Tavern] were the only people Gamble would go see play live."

Like Florida folk icon Frank Thomas, Charlie is pretty much what you see, either off stage or on. "I have to be who I am," he says. "All the other people were taken." Charlie's wit and humor reflect a good-natured approach to life, but he freely admits there was a darker time in his life, when he was wrestling with his own demons and his own mental illness. On stage, he introduces his song "Our Mutual Friend" in autobiographical terms: "Here's a song about a guy who's lived in the same place all his life, and he's just trying to catch his bearings. He's not suicidal by any means, but he's sitting out on this ledge in his underwear, wondering where it all went, so…" and then he sings his beautiful song in sad nostalgic tones and colors:

> *There were clothes hanging out on the line,*
> *The marching band down the street was doing something horribly wrong*
> *To some poor unsuspecting song,*
> *There's wood smoke in the air and summer's gone,*
> *It ain't coming back again,*
> *It's waving goodbye to our mutual friend.*

A follow-up song to Charlie's experiences in mental health is "The Dalai Lama's Birthday," which is about the process of writing songs while still recovering from a psychotic break. "Things went really peculiar, they went sideways, as they say, and I was recovering in the county time-out pen, and I had enormous problems with insomnia," Charlie remembers. "The weird thing is when you go for long periods without sleep, you get these odd, fragmented thoughts that, in fact, sometimes make great song lyrics. There's always that silver lining, see? So I was sitting on the porch, about 104 degrees outside, and my wife was snoring away, God bless her, and the radio guy came on, back when they had radio guys, and he said today's celebrity birthdays were such and such, and he had a few names that ended with His Holiness the Dalai Lama, and this struck me as a very positive thing, and somehow I knew everything was going to be okay." And then he sings:

Lesser hands are reaching out to God,
Equal parts of reverence and dread,
Fearing neither darkness nor the light,
Sleepless in a week of unmade beds.
Not a single star that I can see,
February turns to May and June,
This is sure a slow night in the sky,
Wasn't there supposed to be a moon?
This is the Dali Lama's birthday,
I was hoping for a moon.

For a while, Charlie played in a duo with Don Dunaway, calling themselves Uncle Jubal. The two songwriters resorted to creating duo arrangements via long-distance over the telephone. "There was a lot of stress going on," Don admits. "My marriage was breaking up, and I was really temperamental. It got to the point where if I were to learn a new song, I'd get Charlie to record it for me, and I'd go learn it by myself, and we'd put the song onstage."

But Don has nothing but praise for his old friend and Charlie's skills as a songwriter. "Charlie's songs are southern gothic," Don says. "I've never heard anyone write about the South the way Charlie does."

In fact, one of our favorite Charlie Robertson songs is a bit of old Jacksonville trivia and history: "The Ritz Café: No Line on the Main Floor" is about Charlie McRoy, or as Robertson describes, "this really cool guy," who stood outside the Morrison's Cafeteria (near Hemming Plaza in downtown Jacksonville). McRoy would call out to prospective customers,

Charlie Robertson and the author at the Will McLean Festival in March 2014. *Taken by Janice Niemann, author's collection.*

"No line on the main floor! Short line in the carriage room!" Usually decked out in a white suit with top hat and bow tie, he called out the day's specials. "All you can eat! Turkey dinner, one dollar and twenty five cents! No line on the main floor!" If one of the traditions of folk is reminding us of the characters in our past heritage and culture, this song, with all its humor and nostalgia, captures a slice of Jacksonville history and certainly fits the bill.

Charlie Robertson is doing well these days and continues to perform at a few of the local festivals throughout the state. He appears to be quite comfortable in his own skin, and he remains unassuming, quick to smile and very much a master of the English language. His songs are masterpieces of folklore, and he is a joy to watch in concert. He is too modest to say so himself, but Charlie continues to influence and touch the lives of every musician who crosses his path or who is lucky enough to see him perform. He remains one of the finest folk singers and songwriters in the United States today, and he is without a doubt a living Florida treasure.

11

Frank and Ann Thomas:
The Cracker Cowman Sound

Frank Thomas sits in a rocking chair on the wraparound porch at his house, the Cracker Palace, as he entertains a large number of people who are there to help him celebrate his seventieth birthday. There are family members, musicians, songwriters and friends who have come to extend to the "godfather of Florida folk music" happy birthday and well wishes.

I ask Frank how he's doing. "Oh, I ain't nothin' extree," Frank tells me as he sits back in his big rocker on the porch, "but I'm getting by." The crowd celebrating Frank's birthday is spread out across the porch, spilling out into the yard. Down to the right of us, Emmett Carlisle and a group of musicians have broken into a song about Louis Payne, a Florida resident who was involved in the Lincoln assassination and later hanged for it. Frank listens and nods his head, giving his approval.

"Son, you've justified your existence," he half-jokes after the song is over. Emmett beams, because like most Florida folk musicians, he knows that this is Frank's way of giving them his much-welcome seal of approval, and it is music to their ears.

Frank's family members get together for a group picture on the porch. At seventy, Frank is the youngest of a long line of siblings, and most of his immediate family is gone now, but Frank has a slew of cousins, aunts and uncles and now great-grandnieces and nephews and the like. "I have first cousins that, if they had lived, would be over a hundred years old," Frank said. One of his great-great-great-nephews, twenty-three-year-old Eroc Hendel, is sitting on the porch with guitar in hand, watching the goings-on. Frank's wife, Lisa, is always nearby, making sure things run smoothly and that Frank is OK.

Frank and Lisa Thomas at the Will McLean Festival, March 2014. *Gail Carson Photography.* *Used with permission.*

Later on, when the sun goes down, a little peach-flavored moonshine is passed around—just a sip is all you need. The songs go on well into the evening. It is a great birthday party, and Frank seems fairly satisfied with it all.

To the Florida folk singers of today, Frank Thomas is a legend, and he is "something extree" indeed. Winner of the 1993 Florida Folk Heritage Award (along with his late wife, Ann Thomas), Frank has written hundreds of original songs, most of them about Florida, his beloved home. Like Will McLean, his friend and confidant, Frank has "spread the word" through music and lyrics about his love and concerns for Florida, the land his family has lived on for many generations now. He remembers:

> *When I was born in 1943, my daddy was already up there in years. He carried the mail, and we lived out in the woods near where Camp Blanding is now, a place called Belmore. My dad was born in 1882, and he was a soldier who served in World War I. My grandparents on both sides lived during the Civil War. My great-granddaddy fought at Olustee and in the Seminole War. During the Civil War, he was going to Jacksonville to catch the train to Cold Harbor, Virginia. The only way he could get to*

Jacksonville was riding a horse, so my grandfather, who was ten at that time, rode with him all the way up to Jacksonville. He caught the train, and that was the last time my grandfather ever saw him. He was wounded at Cold Harbor and developed lockjaw. He never made it back.

My mom was a Conway; her family was musical, and her Uncle played guitar. We all lived in that North Florida area around Middleburg. My daddy played a pretty good mouth organ; my uncle played fiddle, and all his children played guitars. His name was Royal Thomas, and he worked out at Raiford Prison. I think he was a warden for a while. He got remarried, and her name was Naomi, and she taught me some of my first guitar chords.

I grew up listening to old country, people like Roy Acuff, Hank Snow, Hank Williams, Webb Pierce and those fellas, that was real country.

He sings out a little verse of his own memory:

I was four or five years old when I first heard that song,
I grabbed an old Prince Albert can and tried to play along,
It was Roy Acuff singing about the Wabash Cannonball,
And thinking back that's when I got the call,
That Country music sure got a hold of me
I was playing at an early age, no more than two or three.

We had a battery-operated radio, and it wasn't until I was twelve or thirteen that we got electricity. My brother had just got back from the Korean War, and up until then we didn't have it. Part of the problem was the Clay Electric Company in Keystone Heights wore green uniforms and the Federal revenuers wore green uniforms, too. When we finally got electrical power, it was amazing to me, almost magical. This was about 1955 or so. They told my daddy it would cost him one or two dollars a month. Then a few months later, he got a bill for ten dollars, and he got so angry he rode his horse to Keystone Heights to complain. "Oh, we made a mistake," they told him. "There's a zero on the end that shouldn't be there, that should be one dollar!"

Before the age of ten, Frank began singing hymns with his family's gospel group. Later, he began to attend square dances, where he learned a little fiddle from a traditional fiddler named Allie Murray. He also received inspiration from his mother, who wrote songs about Florida. "When I was growing up, my mama wrote songs back then. I was thinking about one the other day, a song she wrote called 'Autumn.'" Frank was able to recall a part of it even now: "My favorite season's here/The best time of the year/ Autumn, so colorful, yet life improves with the rain."

Frank is unique in one aspect of his own songwriting in that he never writes them down. "I remember most of them," he says. "Sometimes I'll forget about one for a while, and then later on I'll remember it and play it again. I've just never got into writing them down. I didn't need to!"

He admits he's not always the best judge of what his best songs are. "When I wrote 'Cracker Cowman,' I wouldn't have given a dime for it, but then people said how much they loved it and they kept requesting it. I guess they thought it was a pretty good song." The song "Cracker Cowman" remains one of Frank's most popular songs, and the first verse shows off Frank's songwriting skills:

> *His beard may be stubbled, like a cut-over sugarcane field,*
> *His clothes may be dirty, but the look in his eyes lets you know he won't yield.*
> *He's from a breed that has died, but he has survived, the world that he once knew is gone,*
> *He's an old Cracker Cowman, existing a long way from home.*

> *(Chorus)*
> *Now dirt bikes scream over land that used to be scrub cow trails*
> *And interstate highways have taken the place of old Mr. Flagler's rails*
> *Condos rise from the land and space shuttles fly,*
> *And the old Cracker Cowman don't know how it all passed him by.*

> *I wrote that song after we went out and had dinner with ol' Sam King. Here he was a millionaire, but he wore a couple of day's growth of beard, and he was wearing old worn-out jeans. I asked him if he ever met the legendary Florida Cracker Cowboy Bone Mizell. Sam said that he had met him and that his daddy knew him real well. He thought he was an honest man because he asked him how many rattlers he'd killed. 'About four or five hundred, I reckon,' Bone Mizell told him. 'And how big was the biggest snake you'd ever killed?' 'Oh, about five feet or so.' Any man tells you they've killed four hundred snakes and none of them was over five feet, that's an honest man!*

Life was not easy in those days in North Florida, and Frank determined fairly quickly that farm living was not what he wanted to do. "When I was

Collage of Frank Thomas photos, all taken by Gail Carson. *Gail Carson Photography. Used with permission.*

sixteen, we formed a band and went up to Jacksonville, but that didn't last too long. A few days later, my dad came up and got me. I never did like working the farm, milking cows, plowing with mules, all that sort of thing, so my father gave me an ultimatum."

"You can help me farm or join the military" is what he told me, so at sixteen, almost seventeen, I went into the army. I was stationed in Michigan, but I went to Da Nang in Vietnam for about six months. We set up radios and communication stations for the Special Forces in 1963. It was all hush-hush and covert. The CIA had us sign documents saying we were never there, I don't know how they kept all that secret for so long. When Kennedy was assassinated at the end of 1963, I had just gotten back to the States. We had a lot of down time because we were army radio personnel on an air force base, so I got to play music a lot. In 1964, the rest of the country was into the Beatles, but bluegrass was my thing, and I started playing

with the Taylor Bros, out of Monroe, and through them I hooked up with the Arkansas Travelers.

The Arkansas Travelers had already been around a long time, performing and touring America and Canada since the '30s and '40s, and they were contracted to play the Grand Ol' Opry four times a year, among many other country and bluegrass gigs. In the 1960s, they were looking to modernize their sound so they went electric, and they looked for a drummer and a new front man, someone who could not only sing but write good songs. So they hired me to front the band, and I spent seven years with them on the road. During those years, I did most of the bus driving because I was the only one in the band who had a chauffeur's license. Their agent was out of Savannah, and we recorded something for Mercury Records, I think. Most of these guys were pretty old. The main fella was George Brumley, and he was the youngest member except for me and the drummer, Ronnie Ross. George was Al Brumley's brother, the songwriter who wrote "I'll Fly Away" in 1929. Some of the best shows I ever played were with the Travelers, especially when we played the Grand Ol' Opry in the Ryman Auditorium.

Some people talk about the glamorous life of an entertainer out on the road, but let me assure you, it is not. Except for a few good times, I had had enough of it after six or seven years, and I eventually came back to Middleburg. I worked for a while with a friend of mine who had a tree pushing business. It was steady work, and they paid me $300 a week to push trees over, which was more than I was making playing music. That's how I ended up in Lake Wales. Six or seven months later, I got a letter from the Arkansas Travelers, who had regrouped, and since I was still legally under contract, they insisted I join them for some shows up in Bronson, Missouri, which I did. When the group broke up again, I got out of my contract and left the Arkansas Travelers for good.

I first met Will McLean in passing while we were in Nashville. We hit it off since we're both from Florida, but we didn't play any music back then. Later on, we reconnected when we both had returned home to Florida, and we started playing a little bit, and I got to know him better. I remember I was impressed because he could drink more than anyone I knew, but my God, the man had a voice!

Living in Lake Wales, I used to go and play at Carl Allen's Historical Café and Catfish House. Carl advertised himself as a real Florida Cracker, and he was quite proud of it. He was a friend of then–Democratic candidate Lawton Chiles, who was running for governor of the state, and I got to know Lawton pretty well. All the local musicians

*would play at Carl's, and word got out about us so we started drawing
a big crowd!*

*I met Ann at one of these shows; she was writing for a newspaper then.
I had already written my first Florida song, "My Heart Is Buried in This
Florida Sand." I got that phrase from Carl when we offered him an emcee
(master of ceremonies) job in Alabama, but he turned us down flat, saying
he would never leave Florida. I wrote another song, "Jamming at Catfish
Carl's," which got some airplay on the local radio station. Soon after that,
Ann picked up bass, and we started to play music together. When I was
doing my album for the Great Southern Label, I wrote* Florida Stories, *and Ann joined me on a few of the songs there. She played bass and added
some "oohhs" and "ahhhs"; she could hit those high notes. We had people
from the Bellamy Brothers and the Nitty Gritty Dirt Band drop by. Pearly
Curtis from the Dirt band was listening to some playback and asked us
would we mind if he added a little dobro on to one of the songs. I told him
we couldn't afford him, but he brushed that off, and I think he ended up
playing on several tracks for that album. I told him I'd pay him later, but I
never could find him after that.*

*I started playing with Paul Champion around that time. Paul was
well known for his banjo work with the Folksters, but he was also a
master on the guitar. He never said a word on stage, but my God, what
a musician. Paul played some on the album, and when it was released,
the song "The Battle of Olustee" went to number one on radio stations
in Pensacola and Jacksonville. Back then, BMI would collect monies
for artists and small markets, and I got a pretty good royalty check from
foreign airplay. When I called BMI and asked them about it, they said
most of it came from Canada!*

We were contracted with Great Southern for our Florida Stories
*album, but after that we set up our own recording company. We became
Olustee Records and Ocean Pond Music Publishing Company; this was all
in the '70s. When BMI changed their way of collections, I didn't see much
point in maintaining all that. I used to copyright everything, but I haven't
done that in years, I figure what's the point? If someone wants to record it,
I figured they'd let me know.*

While Frank and Ann were beginning to play out more across the state,
not everyone in his family approved of the type of music they were doing. "I
remember I called a cousin of mine in St. Augustine, and told him Ann and
I were thinking about coming by and paying them a visit. He asked me why

I was going to be in St. Augustine, and I told him we were playing the first Gamble Rogers festival, I forget what year that was, and I told him we were playing folk songs about Florida and all. 'I'd heard that!' my relative told me over the phone. 'I had hoped it wasn't true. I guess you can't expect everyone in the family to turn out good!' Needless to say, we didn't go by for a visit."

Frank and Ann continued to play gigs and festivals and record songs and albums through their Olustee Label, including albums like *Spanish Gold*, *Just Another Day* and *Bingo! The Fourth Seminole War*. "We were performing with Gamble Rogers, Will McLean, Paul Champion and Jim Ballew," Frank told us. "It was a great time to play music in Florida."

Frank met civil rights advocate and Jacksonville resident Stetson Kennedy through Gamble Rogers, and the two men immediately hit it off. "I knew about Stetson before I met him, but I thought he was dead," Frank admits.

> *I went over and introduced myself, and we became good friends after that. He had a lot of stories about the WPA, he was Zora Thurston's boss there, and they did some recording with Alan Lomax. I wrote a song about Stetson that he seemed to like OK. You know he wrote that book* The Klan Unmasked, *and he did those radio shows back then under the name "Superman," which nearly got him killed. He was a good man."*
>
> *Ann and I were married in 1979. She always had this competitive side to her, and she started writing her own songs and right away there were some good ones. "Lost Tourist's Letter Home" was the first one she wrote, I think."*

It goes:

> *I was headed for Miami on a Greyhound out of Boston,*
> *I was bound for the surf and the sun,*
> *But I got off by mistake*
> *In a place called "The Scrubbin'"*
> *Now I wonder, what have I done?!*
>
> *(Chorus)*
> *Hey Mom, they fish in their prairies and their ponds ain't got no water,*
> *And the Ocean's fifty miles from this town,*
> *Their turtles are called "cooters" and their tortoises are "gophers"*
> *And who, I wanna know, is Parson Brown?!*

Ann Thomas worked in Lake Wales as the city's main public librarian, and she was very much involved with children's reading and literacy programs for many years. Sometimes Ann would get into trouble for speaking her mind, but she was widely known and respected for being her own woman.

"She was a case," Frank's eyes twinkle as he tells the story. "She started wearing overalls. Ann wore these Seminole skirts back when we first started performing, but one time, the dark stage reflected up and she actually got sunburned all over her legs and her backside. She told me, 'If I can wear these overalls, I won't need to wear a bra and I won't get sunburned on my butt!' So yeah, she always wore overalls after that."

Ann's most beloved song is the classic "Story Teller's Song," which has been recorded by a handful of artists, including Amy Carol Webb and others. "We were riding along late at night, back from Pensacola, and she started making up this song. I told her that's pretty good, she'd better write it down, and she told me, 'You don't write them down! Why should I?!' Sure enough, the next morning she couldn't remember how it went! I think it took her another year to finish it. In the song, a child listens to her grandmother tell about bygone, gentle sirens. The child says she would love to have been living way back then to see such enchanted things. And the child cries, 'Nana, were there ever really manatees?'"

"I've seen six thousand or more people start crying when she sang that final verse about the manatee," Frank admitted. "We finally had to end our sets with it, it was so powerful."

We started hosting a few live shows called "Cracker Saturday Nights," which was sponsored by WMNF-FM in Tampa, and we'd have folks like Gamble, Jim Ballew and Jim Billie, who always did a great show. From that, Ann and I started doing a radio show in the '80s and into the '90s called Songs of Florida. We were on for over a decade every week. I remember asking Gamble Rogers on the show one time, "Gamble, are you a folk singer or an entertainer or a country musician?" and he said, "Frank, I'm a whiskey salesman. Whatever I do on stage, the more whiskey I sell, the more they like me."

Frank and Ann played many years and many shows together, until sadly Ann passed away from cancer in 2009. The Gazebo at the Stephen Foster Park where the Florida Folk Festival is held every year is named in her honor.

Frank paused a moment and said, "Before she died, Ann told me she always thought 'Ancient Voices' was her best song, and sometime after

she passed, Amy Carol Webb recorded it; she did a real good job." Lately, Frank's current wife, Lisa, has taken up singing that song with him on stage. "I'll tell you, I'm glad she does it. She does a fine job with it," Frank smiled.

Frank has mentored so many artists over the years and has picked up the late Cousin Thelma's duties of giving out song assignments to songwriters who come to pay him homage. I myself wrote a song called "Lights Out (1942)" from one such assignment, and it has turned out to be one of my most requested songs. Some songwriters have tried to get Frank to sing songs they've written, but he rarely sings anything he hasn't written himself. "Bobby Hicks and I met at the Florida Folk Festival, and he asked me if I wanted to do this new song he'd written, 'I'm Florida, Need I Say More?' I told him no, he's the one who should do it, and he got angry with me; Bobby had a temper, as you know. We played a lot of music together over the years." Bobby Hicks passed away in 2011. "I still miss him, he was a great artist and a good songwriter."

More recently, Frank has been performing and doing some recording with Ron and Bari Litschauer. "Ron's got a pretty good ear. Bari does, too. They keep up with me pretty well, which isn't all that easy to do sometimes."

"He's great to play music with, of course," Bari Litschauer told me recently at the Will McLean Festival in Brooksville, "but there's no telling what he's likely to play when we get up there on stage. Or even which key to play it in. It's always a challenge, but we love Frank."

Sitting on his front porch, Frank talks about his recently quitting smoking cigarettes, "a hard habit to break." I ask Frank about his health in general. "I've had several heart attacks," he admits. "The last one they had me over at Lakeland Hospital. This was in 2007 or 2008, and Ann was with me when they did a scope, and two of the doctors told me, 'There's not a thing we can do for you, and you only have about two or three weeks to live!' Poor Ann freaked out, and I laid around, feeling sorry for myself and just taking it easy for a couple of weeks, but I thought about it for a while and finally I said 'Bull———!' I went to see my family doctor, the one I've had for years, and he said, 'Don't buy into all that.' And he was right. That was over five years ago. I really thought I'd go before Ann did, but it just didn't turn out that way."

Opposite, top: Frank Thomas with Ron and Bari Litschhauer at the Will McLean Festival in March 2014. *Photo taken by author.*

Opposite, bottom: Eroc Hendl and his great-great-uncle Frank Thomas at the Will McLean Festival in March 2014. *Taken by Janice Niemann, author's collection.*

Frank sits back in his rocking chair as the evening sky begins to turn dark. It is quiet for a moment, and he tells me, "You see me on stage, you see me on this porch, I'm the same, what you see is what you get. I don't see no point in doing it any other way. I am what I am and that's it."

12

The Makley Family:
She Taught Us to Yodel

E very folk scene has its musical families that continue to influence other families over the years as they perform and share their music with fans. Sometimes it is the family groups that have the best harmonies, as they've usually been singing them since they were children. Nationally, the Carter family is perhaps best known, but there are many others, and in Florida, the Makley family has the longest continual run of performances and writing original music.

The Makleys have been performing for over forty years at the Florida Folk Festival and even some years before that in local churches and other venues. Known for their yodeling as well as their singing and songwriting, the Makley family carries on a tradition first established by their mother, Elroyce, who is remembered fondly by many festivalgoers to this day. I myself can still see her clearly, holding onto her autoharp, performing "Wildwood Flower" on the Marble Stage. The climactic moment in their show was always when "Mom" Makley and her daughters hit that triple yodel, sending chills up the spine.

Elroyce Lucinda "Mom" Makley was born on June 9, 1926, and made her first public appearance on the *Ted Mack Original Amateur Hour* TV program around 1962. Billed as "the Yodelin' Housewife," she sang "He Taught Me to Yodel" while she played dobro guitar. It was the beginning of a Florida legacy.

Elroyce's main devotion in her music was to her church, and she sang and played many gospel songs, including many of her own originals. When St. Matthews Catholic Church went "folk" in the '60s, she performed there every Sunday for the folk mass, usually with her young daughters.

Early in 1971, she and her daughters Ruthanne and Bettina initially auditioned for the Florida Folk Festival over the phone for Cousin Thelma Boltin, who liked what she heard and arranged a face-to-face audition in the home of Jay and Peggy Smith in Jacksonville. The Makley's first performance at the FFF was in May 1971. Bettina remembers being enthralled with the park itself. "I was fifteen then, and I was so into what I was doing that I hardly noticed people like Will McLean and Gamble Rogers! Looking back on it now, I came to regret not getting to know them more, and I wrote a song about it, 'I Should Have, Could Have Known You Better.'" Bettina became known for her own remarkable songs over the years, both for the Makleys and on her own solo projects, including Under the Water Lillies. Bettina's songs include "Wooden Angels," "I Choose Love" and her very funny "Big Fat Kitty." She is perhaps best known for her song "White Springs Yodel," which the Makleys usually perform together live in their sets at the Florida Folk Festival:

Beneath the tower under the Florida skies,
We come together for some family harmony,
We bring our music, you bring your musical souls,
They will feel our hearts from Georgia to the Keys.
(Yodel)

Here on the Suwannee among the Florida folks,
Where we all keep Mother Nature company,
We hear music, it stirs our musical souls,
We are glad to share it with the birds and bees.
(Yodel)

When we hear autoharp played on that ol' Marble Stage,
It brings back more than forty years of memories
Of playing music and joining musical souls,
So we may leave our hearts forever in White Springs.

Opposite, top: The Makley family. *Collection of the Makley family and used with permission.*

Opposite, bottom: Elroyce, Bettina and Ruthanne Makley at the 1978 Florida Folk Festival. *Image No. FA3990. State Archives of Florida,* Florida Memory, *http://floridamemory.com/items/show/109909.*

The final bit of yodeling at the end of the song reaches a crescendo that includes some triple and five-part harmony yodeling that usually brings the house down. Other songs the group sings regularly include "He Taught Me to Yodel," Lucindagail Maynard's "(Let's Go Down to) The River" and Ruthanne Mason's "Little Blue Tear Drop Trailer."

The group was once featured in an article about the Florida Folk Festival in *National Geographic Magazine,* and it was also included in the book *Yodel-Ay-Ee-Oooo: The Secret Book of Yodeling Around the World* by Bart Lantanga.

Elroyce Makley, the matriarch of the family, sadly passed away at St. Vincent's Hospital in Jacksonville just before her seventy-seventh birthday on June 7, 2003, only a month or so after her singing partner, "Uncle Ray" Sine, died. Since that time, there have been adjustments to the lineup, as the sisters' own daughters have now grown up and joined in, making the Makleys a multi-generational Florida folk family. Natalie, Sarah and Emily Mason-Patterson have all been included at one time or another in the Makley lineup.

The Makleys have influenced and inspired other family groups over the years, many who have joined the Florida folk roster in the past couple of decades. Today, one is apt to see on the folk festival bill the New '76ers, the Morse Family, Jubal's Kin and Loner's Junction, among others, all Florida families who have taken folk music into their lives and made it their own. Meanwhile, the Makley family continues to perform at the Florida Folk Festival and other venues, keeping "Mom" Makley's dream very much alive, stirring our collective musical soul.

13

Don Grooms: Walk Proud, My Son

Don Grooms was a professor at the University of Gainesville who taught journalism and communications, but he ended up teaching much more than that. His songs about Florida and Indian history were so memorable that anyone who heard them knew right away they were in the presence of a powerful and very talented artist. Don wrote great songs like "Vitachuco" and "Congratulations Standing Bear," which are nothing less than four-minute history dissertations. On stage, Don was an exceptional entertainer, moving from solemn storyteller for one song to a comic the next. His satirical songs, e.g. "Winnebago" or "Draw the Line" (a song about eating anything but liver), were outrageously funny and usually made people laugh out loud. With strong melodies and lyrics that were very clever, it was difficult not to sing along when Don had the stage. Almost twenty years after his death, Don Grooms's songs are still played at the festivals with some regularity, and he remains one of Florida's finest songwriters.

Don Grooms (1930–1998) was born in Cherokee, North Carolina, in Haywood County, the son of Noah Grooms and Lockie Butler Johnson. His life as a young man was hard, as expressed in one of his most popular songs, "Walk Proud, My Son." Don would introduce the song by saying, "My mama was the hardest working, most wonderful woman I know. We lived up in the mountains, thirty-five miles away from the nearest store. She'd feed us and clothe us, all on twelve dollars a month. She'd patch our clothes and tell me that 'we didn't steal them, nobody gave them to us' and to not be ashamed, but to 'Walk Proud.' So I wrote that song for her."

Above: Don Grooms and Chief Jim Billie in the 1980s. *From the collection of Florida Folklife. Image No. FA5827. Used with permission.* State Archives of Florida, Florida Memory, *http:// floridamemory.com/items/show/111606.*

Opposite: Vitachuco meets Hernando de Soto, 1539. *Painting 1906, George Gibbs illustrator. Public domain. Image No. PR02987.* State Archives of Florida, Florida Memory, *http:// floridamemory.com/items/show/2827.*

After serving his country in the Korean War, Grooms acquired academic degrees from Southern Methodist University and UCLA. He honed his skills as a journalist, and over time, Grooms became known as one of the top television/radio/media education experts in the country. An Associated Press war correspondent and a White House reporter, Don eventually took a job as associate professor at the University of Florida and later won the College Broadcasting Teacher of the Year award. He also assisted the Seminole tribe in upgrading its communications department and worked with them on several other projects.

Because of his influence, some of the students who passed through Don's classes went on to become Florida folk singers themselves, including Tom Shed, Peter Gallagher and Al Poindexter, among others. Tom Shed in particular worked closely with Don, his mentor, who had invited Tom over for some Sunday jams. Tom tells us: "Don politely listened to some of my

songs, a few things I was doing at the time, and then he sang his own song, about the Indian chief who battled with de Soto, 'Vitachuco,' and I was blown away. After he was through singing, he looked at me and said, 'Tom, you need to try writing some songs that mean something.'" Eventually, Don and Tom worked together recording Don's only studio release album, *Walk Proud, My Son*. The album was done in 1981 at Modern Music Workshop in Gainesville, Florida, and mastered by Randy Kling in Nashville. Ray Valia was the recording engineer, and Tom Shed (then Tom Sheddan) was the producer. Don recorded two cassette tapes after that but nothing that met the production of his only album with Tom.

Much of Don Grooms's early musical career was spent appearing in Florida music clubs, including the Blue Sink in Hamilton County and the Gator Hook Saloon in the Everglades. "I played wherever they would let me," he liked to say, "and a lot of other places, too." Grooms became a featured performer at festivals across the Southeast, including the Cocoa and Smallwood Store Seminole Festivals. At the 1992 Fire on the Swamp festival, he performed his original song "The Orange Blossom Special Don't Stop in Waldo Anymore" with, of all people, fiddler Chubby Wise, who is still considered by many to be the co-author of the "Orange Blossom Special."

Don Grooms was a fixture at the Florida Folk Festival for over twenty-five years, and he was good friends with Will McLean, Gamble Rogers, Paul Champion and other Florida folk legends. Don was known for his clever compositions, such as "Winnebago" and his own rendition of "Sugar Babe," as well as sensitive ballads regarding the lives of Native Americans with such great songs as "Tsali," including the lyric "Jesus died for you, but Tsali died for me."

Don worked hard against the state's indifference to folk artists at that time, and he inspired many changes in the Florida Folk Festival that led to the creation of the state's public-financed Folk Arts Program. He championed the causes of many young performers who were unable to make the festival lineup and defended the veterans and the old ways he felt the state was allowing to slip away. Using a biting wit that stung as much as it tickled, Don Grooms was not afraid to say what was on his mind. His beliefs and standards were adopted in the formation of the Friends of Florida Folk (FOFF) organization, which monitors the improved state Folk Arts programs.

In 1996, Don Grooms was awarded the Florida Folk Heritage Award, a folk singer's highest honor.

Don passed away two days shy of his sixty-eighth birthday in 1998. A private memorial service hosted by folk singers Frank and Ann Thomas

Don Grooms at the 1988 Florida Folk Festival. *From the collection of Dan Stainer. Image No. FA4739. Used with permission. State Archives of Florida,* Florida Memory, *http://floridamemory.com/items/ show/110616.*

was held on January 17, 1999, at Gore's Landing, near Silver Springs. He is buried in North Carolina, near his home where he was raised as a child.

A few years ago, I made a special visit to see my good friends Jerry and Lynnis Mincey, who have a beautiful home up on Cold Mountain near Cherokee, North Carolina. While I was there, Jerry and I made a visit to Don's grave high up on a tall hill, overlooking the beautiful North Carolina countryside. We found his resting site, alongside those of several of his relatives, and after burning a little sage, we broke out our guitars and played a few of Don's songs. Maybe it was just me, but I swear at one point we all had a nice three-part harmony going on "Walk Proud, My Son."

14

Dale Crider: Keeping Florida Green

On a mild November evening, in a concert hall at the Flamingo Lake RV Park in Jacksonville, Florida, a crowd of about one hundred or so people grew quiet as Mr. Dale Crider, a well-known and beloved Florida folk singer and environmentalist, approached the microphone slowly, with some obvious effort. After two weeks of being bedridden with the flu, he appeared thin and pale. Those closest to him by the stage watched him anxiously, wondering if at any moment he might teeter and fall over like a big pine tree.

"I almost didn't make it tonight," he spoke, and the room grew even quieter. Then he grinned and said cheerfully, "But you make me glad I did."

The room erupted once more into loud applause. To the festival promoters and North Florida Folk Network officers, it was amazing Dale Crider was even there at all. After two days of music and good times, the climax of the festival was their presentation of an award to Dale for Florida Folk Artist of the Year. They were told, up to the last minute, he "most likely wouldn't be able to make it" and had resigned themselves that his honorarium would be awarded in absentia. Fortunately, to the surprise of just about everyone, Dale had managed to make the ninety-minute drive up to Jacksonville, and now, unexpectedly, here he was.

Dale Crider was being honored by the North Florida Folk Network (NFFN) on that day for his fifty years of performing Florida folk music and also for fighting for the environment as few men in Florida ever had. For over thirty years, Dale worked within the system, a biologist with the Florida Fish and Wildlife Commission, educating the public on environmental issues and concerns, working to preserve what he knew might one day be lost forever.

Collage of Dale Crider photos taken by Gail Carson. *Gail Carson Photography. Used with permission.*

Many of the folks in the audience that night were aware that even then, Dale was currently involved in a legal battle between the States of Georgia and Florida as they argued over which had the right to control the flow of the Apalachicola River into the Gulf. For Dale, fighting for Florida's unique environment remains a battle that has no end.

His body weakened, but his spirits bright, Dale Crider stood on this wooden stage in Jacksonville, humbly accepting the NFFN award and honorarium, along with the NFFN Festival poster, signed by all the participants of the two-day gathering. The crowd's applause and obvious outpouring of love lifted his mood, and he decided he would say a few words, maybe even play a song or two.

He grinned and began to talk about getting started in the folk music scene over half a century ago. "The Florida Folk Festival started about the same time I did, around 1953," he said. "Even then we knew the power of folk songs and how music influences people. Folk music is a great teacher. I was inspired by Will McLean, and after a while I knew I had to start doing my own songs. Finally, one day I managed to write 'The Mangrove Buccaneer,' and suddenly I was a Florida folk song writer!"

The audience watched as Dale took his guitar out of the case and began to strum. The guitar wasn't exactly in tune, but no matter; in folk music, the song's the thing, and Dale, the ultimate showman, wanted to give the crowd what they had come for. He managed to sing "I'm the Mangrove Buccaneer" with as much gusto as his exhausted body would allow, and he seemed to grow visibly stronger as the audience joined in on the chorus.

Dale was grinning broadly at the song's end as the audience enthusiastically applauded. His spirits obviously lifted, Dale was able to talk for almost an hour on what he loved best: nutrition and routes to better health by eating naturally. He told the group he loved to look for certain Florida grasses every morning and churn them up into a morning drink, suggesting it was "one of the healthiest things you'll ever know." He talked about the many varieties of food available in everyday flora. "Fresh chlorophyll is especially important to the human body. Getting away from the big food corporations who are bleaching and removing all the natural positive effects of foods is imperative for good health," he said. "And you don't have to take my word for it, do the research!"

Finally he sang his most popular song, "Apalachicola Doin' Time," and the audience joined in, the chorus growing louder every time it came around.

> *Apalachicola River water*
> *Is the veins of our land,*
> *Alligators in her swampy borders*
> *Are a part of nature's plan.*
> *Give the word to protect her*
> *Call the technical sector*
> *Soften up the cry to drain the swampland dry*
> *Apalachicola let her wind*
> *Apalachicola strong in mind*
> *Apalachicola flowin' fine, Lord,*
> *Apalachicola doin' time!*

Dale Crider ended his set to a warm, standing ovation. NFFN directors Larry Mangum and Ray Lewis greeted Dale on stage and thanked everyone for coming out to the festival. Dale was feeling good about the evening, and before he headed for home himself, he greeted a few well-wishers after the show.

Left: Dale Crider, 1977. *Florida Folklife collection. Image No. FA3931. Used with permission. State Archives of Florida,* Florida Memory, *http://floridamemory.com/items/show/109851.*

Opposite: "Ranger" Dale Crider at the 1972 Florida Folk Festival. *Florida Folklife collection. Image No. FA3934. Used with permission. State Archives of Florida,* Florida Memory, *http://floridamemory.com/items/show/109854.*

"Dale Crider is a folk singer who walks the walk," Bob Patterson told me. "More than anyone else, Dale Crider is Florida's greatest environmental troubadour." As both singer and scientist, Dale has made his case before people of all ages that Florida wildlife habitats and the plants and animals that are dependent on them should be saved.

Over these many years, Dale has performed his songs in almost every state of the union and in Argentina, Paraguay, Canada, Australia and the Caribbean. He has performed on stage with Tom T. Hall, the Bellamy Brothers, Nitty Gritty Dirt Band, Gamble Rogers, Will McLean, John Hartford and various other folk, country and bluegrass artists. He has entertained governors and various policymakers from Tallahassee to Washington.

Dale has been interviewed by ABC's Ted Koppel and has performed on various national broadcast and cable networks. You can hear some of Crider's songs in the *World of Audubon* TV specials, TBS's environmental specials and several movies and documentaries on Florida.

These days, Dale prefers to be at home, his beloved Anhinga Roost. His land is in Windsor, a rural community about ten miles from the University of Florida, mostly owned by the St. Johns River Water Management District. Dale's lands include over thirty acres under Newnan's Lake and over sixty acres surrounding it. The difference in Crider's life these days is that he's actually living what he used to teach. "The things I learned while working

Florida Wildlife Boys performing at the Florida Folk Festival, 1960. *From left*: Bob Phillips, Hewey Clemmons and Dale Crider. *Image No. FA3930. Used with permission. State Archives of Florida*, Florida Memory, *http://floridamemory.com/items/show/109850.*

Dale Crider and Red Henry. *Gail Carson Photography. Used with permission.*

with the government, I've been able to put to good use here," he tells us. Dale maintains a significant archaeological find on his land with over 140 ancient canoes, some of them dating back thousands of years, that was discovered some years ago in the mud around Newnan's Lake. Dale refers to the canoes as a connection to the early people of Florida, a connection that Dale feels deeply.

"Nothing lasts forever," he reminds us. "People think they'll be able to maintain oil and petroleum to drive their cars around until the end of time," he smiles, "and they won't. One day soon, things are going to change, and either we'll get back to the things that the ancients knew or eventually we'll die off, like the dinosaurs. We can't maintain this sort of thing for very long before it collapses on itself."

This year, Dale will be honored at the Florida Folk Festival for over fifty years of performing his music there. Looking back on his musical career dating back to 1964, Crider is pleased with some of the progress and the changes of perception he's seen. "Marshes used to be considered ugly, stinky water," he says. "Now it's pretty widely known a swamp is a natural machine, connected to massive filtration systems and life cycles of innumerable habitat." The father of six and grandfather of four is generally optimistic, but he admits he still worries about the future. "People are only just beginning to understand,'" he says, strumming his guitar slowly, "but we're still losing Florida. I'm using education and music to help save what they can," he smiles, "one song at a time."

15

The Future of Florida Folk Music

G amble Rogers and Paul Champion are gone now, but on any given weekend a visitor can walk down the streets of St. Augustine and catch the distinct sounds of Bob Patterson over at O.C. White's or the amazing Sam Pacetti over at the Milltop. In Jacksonville, Art Schill's Saki Shop is only a memory, and the Malabar no longer features top-notch bluegrass music as it once did, but Ray Lewis continues to bring music to such venues as the Mudville Grille. There one can listen to the superb voice and music of Larry Mangum, perhaps doing one of his songwriter's circles or performing with the Peyton Brothers. Over in Tallahassee, the great Del Suggs can sometimes be seen at Bullwinkle's, or perhaps Bill Wharton, aka "the Sauce Boss," will be cooking up some hot licks and gumbo down at the Moon or even the old black club, Smitty's. In Gainesville, Don Grooms is gone, but folks like Tom Shed keep his memory alive every time they climb up on a stage and perform "Vitachuco" or "Walk Proud, My Son." Elsewhere in the state, folk singers and acts like '60s folk legend Rod McDonald, folk duo Bill and Eli Perras and Grant Peeples are continuing the tradition of Will McLean and his old friend Pete Seeger, singing songs that raise the political consciousness and awareness of their audiences.

Every year, there are a number of folk festivals in the state of Florida where literally hundreds of artists compete with one another for a coveted spot on stage, a brief twenty-five-minute set to entertain and pass their message to the crowds. The Will McLean Festival, held annually just before spring, evokes his name as musicians and songwriters gather to honor the man who is responsible for their musical vocation. The Gamble Rogers

Festival, usually held in St. Augustine the first weekend in May, is filled with artists from all over the state who specialize in a fingerpicking style to remember the man who touched their hearts and souls and to teach others about his talents and greatness. In the south region of the state, they honor the great songwriter Steve Blackwell with a festival in his name. The South Florida Folk Festival is also held in this area of the state. The granddaddy of all the Florida festivals, the Florida Folk Festival is still held every year in White Springs along the banks of the Suwannee River (usually Memorial Day weekend), and it remains a three-day celebration of not only the finest in Florida folk music on half a dozen stages but also many other folklore specialties, cultures and crafts.

The Will McLean Foundation has featured a "Best New Florida Folk Song" for many years now for both Florida and out-of-state residents, and the Gamble Rogers Festival promotes its "I Remember Gamble" stage as a storyteller and songwriting venue. Over at the Florida Folk Festival, young children and folks of all ages are participating in the best fiddler's and banjo contests, and almost all the festivals promote new artists and entertainers as much as possible.

Will Florida folk music, as we know it today, survive? As of this writing, the songs of Will McLean, Don Grooms and Gamble Rogers are still being played and sung by old and new artists alike. People like Frank Thomas, Bob Patterson, Charlie Robertson, Tom Shed, Larry Mangum, the Makleys and Dale Crider are still out there, playing their music as they have always done, keeping their own rich, historical traditions alive. Sharing the stages with the old guard are new artists, such as Jubal's Kin, Bing Futch, Aaron O'Rourke, the Morse Family and so many others who are bringing fresh faces and new music to the Florida folk scene.

What has always made (and continues to make) Florida different from the national folk scene is its emphasis on Florida history, its culture and specifically conservation issues, especially regarding the state of Florida itself. The struggle to keep Florida "green" and out of the hands of unscrupulous developers remains a constant battle. We have seen in the past where folk music has made a difference and raised awareness to such levels as to save certain areas of the state from unchecked development, but many would agree they are fighting what often seems to be a losing battle.

Will McLean once described the Florida of his youth as "pristine," a place where a person could drink, swim and fish from the many lakes and rivers that dotted the North Florida region. A large portion of the Florida that his generation grew up with is now gone. In areas Gamble Rogers called his

Above: Collage of current Florida folk singers, all taken by Gail Carson. *Gail Carson Photography. Used with permission.*

Left: Carillon Tower at the Stephen Foster State Park in White Springs. *Robert Leahey, photographer. Image No. FT14108. Used with permission. State Archives of Florida,* Florida Memory, *http://floridamemory.com/items/show/124249.*

"sacred places," they are draining the water to build houses and golf courses, and the Florida his ancestors knew has changed forever. And if Stephen Foster ever did visit the Suwannee River, he certainly wouldn't recognize it today, for it is incapable of supporting any significantly sized steamboat that Foster would have traveled on. The "healing sulfurs" of White Springs that used to attract visitors from all over the world are now a thing of the past, something for curious visitors to read about on education boards, put up by local history clubs and located around the town.

In the footsteps of Will McLean, most Florida folk singers realize that, as they entertain, they have a responsibility to increase awareness of Florida's history and culture and to educate others on conservation issues. It may not be top ten material or get you a contract in Nashville, but it is necessary for the survival of Florida itself. Saving Florida through music is an ideal and a noble cause, the cause of Will McLean, Gamble Rogers, Frank Thomas and Dale Crider. As long as it continues to be the cause of Florida folk musicians and singers, it will remain not just folk music but also folk music with a purpose.

Music with a purpose is what folk music is all about. Saving Florida is what Florida folk music is all about, and as long as that is its purpose and goal, Florida folk music, as we know it, will survive and flourish.

Appendix A

The Top 100 Florida Folk Songs
of All Time

The order and rank of these songs are purely the opinion of the author and have nothing to do with actual recording sales of any kind.

1. "I'm Florida, Need I Say More?" by Bobby Hicks
2. "Old Folks at Home (Way Down Upon the Swanee River)" by Stephen Foster
3. "Cracker Cowman" by Frank Thomas
4. "Lord, Hold Back the Waters (of Lake Okeechobee)" by Will McLean
5. "The Orange Blossom Special" by the Rouse Bros/Bill Monroe/ Johnny Cash
6. "The Story Teller" by Ann Thomas
7. "Lullaby of the Rivers" by Bob Patterson
8. "The Rose and the Gold" by Mem Semmes
9. "Plumes" by Steve Blackwell
10. "Ain't It Great to Be Alive (And Be in Florida)?" by Larry Mangum
11. "Seminole Wind" by John Anderson
12. "(Com'on Down to) The Sunshine State" by Grant Peeples
13. "Apalachicola Doin' Time" by Dale Crider
14. "White Springs Yodel" by Bettina Makley
15. "Doris" by Gamble Rogers
16. "Paw Prints in the Sand" by Ken Skeens
17. "Song for Gamble (When Gamble played That Old Guitar)" by Charley Simmons

18. "Vitachuco" by Don Grooms
19. "A Part of Me/White Springs" by Jeanie Fitchen
20. "Wild Hog" by Will McLean
21. "Barberville" Brian Smalley
22. "Harry T. Moore " by Bill & Eli Perras
23. "The Creek" by Paul Garfinkel
24. "Withlachoochee Way" by Dawn DeWitt
25. "The Last Train Out of Key West" by Boomslang Swampsinger
26. "Hemmingway's Hurricane" by Doug Spears
27. "Sea of Turtle Tears" by Amy Carol Webb
28. "Osceola's Last Words" by Will McLean
29. "The Sandhill Crane and Will McLean" by Gail Carson
30. "Alabama Jacks" Peter Roads Swamp Band (with Boomslang Swampsinger)
31. "The Sinkhole Song" by Lucky Mud
32. "Florida Moon" by Charley Groth
33. "Old Hickory's Town" by Tom Shed
34. "Florida Pines" by Paul Garfinkel
35. "The Ballad of Bone Mizell" by Steve Blackwell
36. "Rand-McNally Map of Florida" by Jim Bickerstaff
37. "Barefoot Mailman" by Emmett Carlisle
38. "Mangrove Buccaneer" by Dale Crider
39. "Florida State of Mine" by Tom Shed
40. "Winnebago" by Don Grooms
41. "Riding the Orange Blossom Trail (Haulin' Oranges!)" by Jerry Mincey
42. "Song for Our Children" by Mary Ann DiNella
43. "Lost Tourist's Letter Home" by Ann Thomas
44. "Battle of Olustee" by Frank Thomas
45. "Old River Road" by Ken Skeens
46. "Tate's Hell" by Will McLean
47. "Zachariah Creech" by Bobby Hicks
48. "Ritz Café (No Line on the Main Floor)" by Charlie Robertson
49. "Roll On Manatee" by Jim Ballew
50. "The West Florida Waltz" by Joe Virga
51. "Mother of Miami (Ballad of Julia Tuttle)" by Cindy Bear
52. "A Hurricane's A-Coming" by Del Suggs
53. "My Florida" by Susan Brown
54. "Turn Back Time" by James Hawkins

55. "Florida" by Larry Mangum
56. "Big Alligator" by Chief Jim Billie
57. "This Florida Again" by Garrison Doles
58. "Spanish Gold" by Frank Thomas
59. "Pickin' Oranges" by J.U. Lee
60. "Ode to Whitey Markle" by Goody Haines
61. "Our Wild Florida" by Dan Gribbin
62. "Shadow of the Hawk" by Al Scortino
63. "The Last Troubadour" by Larry Mangum
64. "Swamp Witch" by Jim Stafford
65. "The Saga of Louis Powell Payne" by Emmett Carlisle
66. "I Could Have, Should Have Known You Better" by Bettina Makley
67. "Let the Rivers Run Free" by Bill and Eli Perras
68. "The Ghost of the Orange Blossom Special" by J.D. Lewis
69. "Bolita Sam" by Don Grooms
70. "Florida Souvenirs" by Ron and Bari Litschauer
71. "Rescue Train" by Ron Johnson and Mary Mathews
72. "My Florida Home" by Frank Thomas
73. "The Boat" by Jerry Mincey
74. "The Day the Ashley Gang Went Down" by Al Scortino/The Ashley Gang
75. "My Heart Is Buried in the Florida Sand" by Frank Thomas
76. "Pigs in My Garden (Again)" by Ron Johnson and Mary Mathews
77. "Ain't Florida Neat?" by Mindy Simmons
78. "Graveyard of the Armadillo" by Grant Livingston
79. "Tamiami Trail" by Peter Gallagher
80. "Somewhere South of Georgia" by Al Scortino
81. "You Can Still See Florida" by Rog Lee
82. "St. Augustine" by Joe Mark
83. "The Ghost of Will McLean" by Larry Mangum
84. "Willie Green Blues" by Bill and Eli Perras
85. "Waking Up in White Springs" by Amy Carol Webb
86. "Florida Girl" by Terry Kelly
87. "Florida Sunshine" by Kate Carpenter
88. "Ancient Voices" by Ann Thomas
89. "Song of the Old St. Johns" by Joe and Katie Waller (Jackson Creek)
90. "Music Drifts Along This River" by Mike Jorgensen
91. "I Love Florida" by Patrick Barmore
92. "Major F. Dade" by James Hawkins

Collage of musical instruments all taken by Gail Carson. *Gail Carson Photography.* *Used with permission.*

Another collage of musical instruments all taken by Gail Carson. *Gail Carson Photography. Used with permission.*

93. "Girl from Immokalee" by Raiford Starke and Peter Gallagher
94. "Golden Fleece of Tarpon Springs" by Mike Jorgensen
95. "F-L-O-R-I-D-A" by Elisabeth Williamson
96. "Keep Florida Green" by Red Henry
97. "Honeymoon in Palatka" by Mark Smith
98. "That Dirty Little Rat that Ate Orlando" by Valerie C. Wisecracker (Val Caracappa)
99. "(I Will Never Leave) My Florida Home/Paradise" by Warren (Wardog) Vanderplate
100. "Okeechobee Waltz" by Raven-Stands-Alone

Appendix B

Statement of J. L. McMullen

April 21, 2003
To Whom It May Concern:
  My name is John Lavelle (J.L.) McMullen. I was born January 12, 1914, on a family farm located five miles north of Wellborn in Suwannee County, Florida, near the bank of the Suwannee River. The farm was purchased in 1938 by my great-grandfather Levi Johns. Since my marriage in 1935, I have resided at 726 Suwannee Avenue in Live Oak, Florida with my wife Kitty.

  In the 1940s I met Aubrey Fowler (a couple of years my senior) a native of Lafayette Country just across from the Suwannee River. Over the sixty plus years I knew Aubrey, he conveyed to me many times a message he said was passed down to his father from his Grandfather Fowler. He said his grandfather shared a home brew with Stephen Foster at a county store located on State Road 10, now US 90, on the east bank of the Suwannee River. This small store, owned and operated by "Bud" O'Hara, is still located at the same site, however it is dilapidated condition.

  I recently had a conversation with Perry O'Hara, the grandnephew of Dan "Bud" O'Hara, owner of the country store. He shared information with me that was passed down in his family. He said it was told to him that Stephen Foster traveled in a steamboat from the Gulf of Mexico up the Suwannee River. Foster stopped at Ellaville where Bud O'Hara's store was located to chat and sip homemade brew with the locals.

It is noted that according to history, Ellaville was the furthest up stream point on the Suwannee River that steamboats were able to navigate. This gives further credence to the popularity of Dan (Buds) O'Hara's community anecdote.

Sincerely,
(Signed)
J.L. McMullen
Live Oak, Florida

Bibliography and Sources

CHAPTER 1: FLORIDA "FOLK" MUSIC PRIOR TO 1800: SPANISH ROOTS

Fuson, Robert H. *Juan Ponce de León and the Discovery of Puerto Rico and Florida*. Granville, OH: McDonald & Woodward, 2000.

Livingston, Carole Rose. *British Broadside Ballads of the Sixteenth Century: A Catalogue of the Extant Sheets and an Essay*. New York: Garland, 1991.

Morison, S.E. *The European Discovery of America: The Northern Voyages, AD 500–1600*. New York: Oxford University Press, 1971.

Morris, Alton C. *Folk Songs of Florida*. Gainesville: University of Florida Press, 1990.

Pastor, John. "Humans Inhabited New World's Doorstep for 20,000 Years." *University of Florida News*, February 13, 2008.

Peck, Douglas T. *Ponce de León and the Discovery of Florida*. Apple Valley, MN: Pogo Press. 1993.

CHAPTER 2: STEPHEN FOSTER: THE FATHER OF AMERICAN MUSIC

Emerson, Ken. *Doo-Dah! Stephen Foster and the Rise of American Popular Culture*. Boston: Da Capo Press, 1998.

————, ed. *Stephen Foster & Co.: Lyrics of America's First Great Popular Songs*. New York: Library of America, 2010.

Hamm, Charles. *Yesterdays: Popular Song in America*. New York: W.W. Norton, 1979.

McMullen, J.L. Open letter, April 21, 2003. From the private papers of Kelly Green and Peter Gallagher.

Chapter 3: The 1860s to 1900: A Not-So-Civil War

Abel, E. Lawrence. *Singing the New Nation: How Music Shaped the Confederacy, 1861–1865*. Mechanicsburg, PA: Stackpole Books, 2000

Chase, Gilbert. *America's Music: From the Pilgrims to the Present*. Champaign-Urbana: University of Illinois Press, 2000.

Coski, John. *The Confederate Battle Flag: America's Most Embattled Emblem*. Cambridge, MA: Harvard University Press, 2005.

Davis, William C. *The Rogue Republic: How Would-Be Patriots Waged the Shortest Revolution in American History*. New York: Houghton Mifflin Harcourt, 2011.

Chapter 4: Music in Florida from 1900 through World War II

Florida State Parks. "One of America's Oldest and Largest Folk Festivals." http://www.floridastateparks.org/folkfest/history.cfm.

Morris, Alton C. *Folk Songs of Florida*. Gainesville: University of Florida Press, 1990.

Thomas, Frank. Interview with author, September 28–29, 2013.

Chapter 5: Will McLean, the Father of Florida Folk Music

Longhill, Margaret. Interview with author, March 8–9, 2014.

Thomas, Frank. Interview with author, September 28–29, 2013.

CHAPTER 6: ON THE SHOULDERS OF GIANTS WE RIDE: GAMBLE ROGERS

Akers, Michael Gordon. Interview with author, April 2014.

Ansbaucher, Syd. Interview with author, October 2013.

Brio, Nick. "Serendipity Means Newness, Happiness, 7 Boys, 2 Girls, Nylon Strings and Success." *Billboard*, April 1964, 10.

Brown. G. *Colorado Rocks: A Half-Century of Music in Colorado.* Boulder, CO: Pruett, 2004.

Carrick Jim. Interview with author, February 2014.

Gamble Rogers Memorial Foundation. www.gamblerogers.com.

Maher, Jack. "Bitter End (Talent): Here's Lucky Find for Anybody." *Billboard*, November 1963, 16.

Patterson, Bob. Interview with author, February 2014.

Rogers, Maggie. Interviews and conversations with author, September 2013–February 2014.

Thomas, Frank. Interview with author, September 28–29, 2013.

CHAPTER 7: "COUSIN" THELMA BOLTIN AND THE FLORIDA FOLK FESTIVAL

Associated Press. "Florida Folk Festival to Get New Life." *St. Augustine Record*, January 25, 2002. http://staugustine.com/stories/012502/sta_455275.shtml.

Bullard, Johnny. Interview with WSLR, January 14, 2012. http://www.youtube.com/watch?v=HlWcokt9zWg.

Crawford, Ken. Interview with author, April 2014.

Florida Department of State. "Florida Memory." http://www.floridamemory.com.

Makley, Bettina. Interview with author, March 2014.

CHAPTER 8: PAUL CHAMPION, THE WORLD'S GREATEST BANJO PLAYER

Higginbotham, Bob. "Remembering Paul Champion." www.paulchampion.net.

Higginbotham, Mike. Interview with author, April 2014.

Thomas, Frank. Interview with author, September 28–29, 2013.

CHAPTER 9: LULLABY OF THE RIVERS: BOB PATTERSON

Patterson, Bob. *Forgotten Florida Tales*. Charleston, SC: The History Press, 2013.
———. Interview with author, February, 2014.

CHAPTER 10: CHARLIE ROBERTSON: OUR MUTUAL FRIEND

Harmon, Daniel Elton. "Don Oja-Dunaway: The Acoustic Soul of St. Augustine." *The Hornpipe*, 1996. http://www.hornpipe.com/hp/don.htm.
Robertson, Charlie. Interviews with author, March 2013 and March 2014.

CHAPTER 11: FRANK AND THOMAS: THE CRACKER COWMAN SOUND

Thomas, Frank. Interview with author, September 28–29, 2013.

CHAPTER 12: THE MAKLEY FAMILY: SHE TAUGHT US TO YODEL

Lantanga, Bart. *Yodel-Ay-Ee-Oooo: The Secret Book of Yodeling Around the World*. New York: Routledge Press, 2003.
Makley, Bettina. Interviews with author, March–April 2014.
Makley, Ruthanne. Interviews with author, September 2013–February 2014.

CHAPTER 13: DON GROOMS: WALK PROUD, MY SON

Florida Department of State: Florida Folklife Program. "Florida Heritage Award Recipients: Don Grooms." http://www.flheritage.com/preservation/folklife/awards/awardDetails.cfm?id=35.

Gallagher, Peter. "Goodbye to an Old Friend." *Seminole Tribune*, January 23, 1998. http://www.semtribe.com/SeminoleTribune/Archive/1998/jan23/dgrooms.shtml.
———. Interviews with author, 2013–14.
Poindexter, Al. Interviews with author, 2013–14.
Shed, Tom. Interviews with author, 2013–14.
Thomas, Frank. Interviews with author, 2013–14.

Chapter 14: Dale Crider: Keeping Florida Green

Crider, Dale. Interview with author, November 9, 2013.

Chapter 15: The Future of Florida Folk Music

Mangum, Larry. Interview with author, January 15, 2014.

Artist Websites

Dale Crider, http://www.anhingaroost.net
Jubal's Kin, http://www.jubals-kin.com
Loner's Junction, http://lonersjunction.com
Larry Mangum, http://www.reverbnation.com/larrymangum
The Morse Family, http://www.facebook.com/pages/The-Morse-Family-Band/162272102086
Aaron O'Rourke ,http://www.aaronorourke.com
Bob Patterson, http://www.bobandjoline.com

RECORDINGS

Crider, Dale. "Appalachicola Doing Time." *Watersongs and Waterways*. All lyrics by Dale Crider. Ahinga Roost Music Company. 2005.

Makley, Bettina. "White Springs Yodel." *Play That One*. Bettina Makley Music. 2001. Out of print.

Mangum, Larry. "The Ghost of Will McLean." *Most Requested*. Mango Records. Catalogue #700261926339. 2013

McLean, Will. "Away O-ee" and "My Soul Is a Hawk." *Will McLean in Concert at Van Wezel Hall*. Nuages Records, NR04. 1997

Patterson, Bob. "Lullaby of the Rivers." *These Diamonds*. The Will McLean Foundation. 2005.

Thomas, Ann. "Lost Tourist Letter Home." *Just Another Day*.... DashGo Records. Catalogue # B001GJVL6. 2008.

Thomas, Frank. "Cracker Cowman." *Just Another Day*.... DashGo Records. Catalogue #B001GJVL6. 2008.

Index

About the Author

R on Johnson is currently serving as president of the North Florida Folk Network (NFFN), and he writes a semi-daily blog for the *Florida Times-Union* ("Today in Florida History"). He is a regular participant at the Florida Folk Festival, Barberville and the Will McLean Festivals, and he writes and records his own original songs, many of them about

Photo by Janice Niemann.

Florida. He won the 2011 Will McLean Song of the Year with his tune "Rescue Train" and has won several song contests in Fernandina and St. Augustine. Ron graduated from Forrest High School in Jacksonville (1971) and later graduated from Florida State University in 1986 with a master's in social work. He currently works in Jacksonville as a licensed clinical social worker.